...BUT
I'M NOT
RACIST!

TOOLS FOR WELL-MEANING WHITES

KATHY OBEAR, ED.D.

The Difference Press

McLean, VA, U.S.A.

Published 2017

ISBN13: 9781683092025

ISBN10: 1683092023

DISCLAIMER

Throughout this book, I have used examples and stories from coaching clients and workshop participants. To ensure their privacy and maintain confidentiality, I have changed their names and any defining details. All of my own personal examples are described as I remember them.

Cover Design: Jennifer Stimson

Editing: Cynthia Kane

Author's photo courtesy of Shannon Acton

Graphics prepared by Pamela Graglia and used with permission of authors

ADVANCE PRAISE

"I love this book! Kathy Obear brings years of experience, personal practice, and perceptive clarity to this accessible handbook for well-meaning whites struggling to understand how we inadvertently perpetuate racial inequity.... *But I'm NOT Racist* addresses both our 'heads' and our 'hands' and is an invaluable guide that lends itself to virtually any context. In my work, I am consistently asked, 'But what can I do?' Recommending this book will be now my first response."

- *ROBIN DIANGELO, PH. D., AUTHOR OF* WHAT DOES IT MEAN TO BE WHITE *AND* WHITE FRAGILITY.

"...*But I'm NOT Racist!* is a very useful and much needed book filled with tools, insights, and suggestions for reclaiming our integrity and becoming better racial justice allies in our organizations and in our communities.:

- *PAUL KIVEL,* AUTHOR OF UPROOTING RACISM: HOW WHITE PEOPLE CAN WORK FOR RACIAL JUSTICE.

"With great insight and compassion, Kathy's brutally honest book uses her own process of unlearning racism to offer an extraordinary roadmap for other whites seeking to do the same. She provides an abundance of useful examples and tools for individual and organizational change. If you're a white person, you need to read this book!"

- *DIANE J. GOODMAN, ED. D., AUTHOR OF* PROMOTING DIVERSITY AND SOCIAL JUSTICE: EDUCATING PEOPLE FROM PRIVILEGED GROUPS.

"At some point, the words ...*But I'm NOT Racist!* have echoed in the thoughts of many white people. Yet, many of us don't know what to do next. Dr. Obear untangles what can be complicated and stressful interactions through personal anecdotes. Whether you are starting or continuing your journey of being better change agents, this book will provide you with tangible next steps."

- *MAURA CULLEN, ED. D., AUTHOR OF* 35 DUMB THINGS WELL-INTENDED PEOPLE SAY.

"I am grateful to Kathy Obear for turning her experiences into stories that teach white people how to engage race dynamics healthfully, effectively, courageously, and humbly. This book provides many insights and practical tips that can help move us out of the paralysis generated from the fear of making an error. Kathy's gift is her ability to offer tools that support us to speak up and use our voice to challenge racism while simultaneously building relationship with those we want to influence. This is a must-have resource for white people who want support in order to take the next step in their journey toward racial justice!"

- *SHELLY TOCHLUK, ED. D., AUTHOR OF* WITNESSING WHITENESS: THE NEED TO TALK ABOUT RACE AND HOW TO DO IT.

"Dr. Kathy Obear has written an insightful book that calls for white people to be brave in confronting resurgent racism in the US. Using her own journey as a white change agent, Obear provides practical action-oriented tips for how to change the world for the better, one intervention at a time."

- *PAT GRIFFIN, ED. D., PROFESSOR EMERITA UNIVERSITY OF MASSACHUSETTS AMHERST AND CO-AUTHOR OF* TEACHING FOR DIVERSITY AND SOCIAL JUSTICE

"In ...*But I'm not racist! Tools for well-meaning whites*, Kathy Obear takes the reader step-by-step in understanding ourselves, our actions, and how we assess and alter each of those. What a tool Kathy is giving us at a time when our steadfast efforts are even more essential. Gone are the days when we can say, "But I didn't mean it like that! I'm not a racist!" We don't have time to be caught in that trap. We have too much work to do in addressing the systemic white supremacy that is becoming ever more visible."

- *FRANCES E. KENDALL, PH. D., AUTHOR OF* DIVERSITY IN THE CLASSROOM AND UNDERSTANDING WHITE PRIVILEGE: CREATING PATHWAYS TO AUTHENTIC RELATIONSHIPS ACROSS RACE.

DEDICATION

In deep gratitude for all who came before and for all who
carry the light of truth and healing today.

Together, we rise.

TABLE OF CONTENTS

INTRODUCTION

I get it. I remember when the worst thing I could ever imagine happening was to be called racist by a person of color, especially if they were a colleague of mine. I grew up believing racists were people in the KKK who terrorized and killed people of color in the name of White Power and White Supremacy. I saw them as evil and wanted nothing to do with them. And believed I was nothing like them. Instead, I was committed to making a difference with my life by helping others and teaching about diversity. I believed I was doing my part—well, actually far more than my part—to create a better world.

That illusion was blown up in 1997 when I had a deeply shattering experience at an intensive Development Lab for organizational consultants. I had been a consultant in this firm for about 5 years. The organization was expanding its business and needed more trainers as well as "deans" of workshops. As one of five consultants who were invited to try out to be some of these new deans, I led a small team of participants as a trial run to test my capacity for leadership. There were about 50 people participating in the Development Lab, including a couple colleagues of color with whom I worked in my own training business.

I thought everything was going well, and I was successfully demonstrating my competence and capacity as a leader. Then my world blew up. I remember the exact moments I felt terrified people would think I was racist and a fraud. I received very clear, very direct negative feedback from two different people of color: one who was the top leader of the Development Lab and one colleague on her team who was assigned as my coach in the experience. In both cases, I was completely shocked and caught off guard when they each confronted me on different occasions about some of my behaviors they experienced as racist. In both instances, they felt I had disrespected their level of authority and not followed their directions. In addition, when I had disagreed with them, they experienced my tone and approach as if I thought they were my peers rather than the leaders of the workshop. They challenged me to consider if I would have treated them in these same ways if they had been white. And when they asked me to take a look at how my racist implicit bias was fueling my racist behavior, all I could hear was their calling me a racist. Somehow, and don't ask me how, I got through the rest of the Development Lab, but I was barely holding myself together. I was in such deep guilt, shame, and embarrassment, and I didn't know what to do.

I was devastated and terrified I had blown my chances of ever working with this consulting firm again or with any of the other 50 participants in that training. I was terrified I had destroyed my reputation as a diversity trainer. I had built my entire life around my identity as a social justice consultant. Who would I be if I lost this? I agonized over the fear that I would have to find a new line of work and had no idea what in the world that could be.

I didn't talk about this traumatic experience with anybody for almost 3 years except my partner and, once, with a white mentor who had been at the event. I spent three very painful years spinning in this dysfunctional pool of shame, fear, and self-recrimination. I hid this situation even from other friends and colleagues with whom I frequently worked. I isolated myself and tried to figure it out on my own, believing I didn't deserve anyone's help.

As I look back, I feel deeply sad about how I wasted those years. If I had only reached out to other white people for support, I might have moved much more quickly through this deeply painful process. I might have been much more useful in my work and been able to help other whites in their journeys. But I was running from the truth, afraid to look in the mirror and acknowledge the depth of racist bias and beliefs I held onto. I believed if I buried this memory and kept moving fast, I would be fine. I knew I was smart and could figure out how to act in front of people of color as well as learn what to say and how to say it so I would never be called racist again. As always, we reap what we sow, and through my actions I created artificial, surface relationships with colleagues of color and kept my distance from other white people by trying to make myself look good at their expense. And I thought everything was fine.

So, I know the deep fear of being called racist and all the horrific fallout we imagine will happen next. The irony is, I actively participated in creating my own isolation. There were always many people around me who would have met me more than halfway if I had chosen the path of courage and authenticity, instead of fear and shame.

If you are like me, I hope you realize you are not alone. I meet so many white people who think they are well-intentioned and believe they work harder than other whites to create inclusive organizations. And like me, they are shocked and devastated if a person of color calls them on their racist behaviors. We're afraid of damaging our relationships with people of color and concerned about our reputation in the organization. Unfortunately, how we react often contributes to making our fears a reality. We more often get defensive when confronted and only focus on our good intent, insisting we didn't mean to cause any harm. We cite our credentials and past accomplishments to try to prove we couldn't have said or done anything that was racist. And we can sometimes feel so angry and resentful someone raised concerns about our behaviors that we judge and criticize the person of color for being too sensitive and over-reactive.

Once we are confronted, we tend to walk on eggshells and keep a low profile for fear of being accused of saying anything else racist. We sometimes feel we are "damned if we do, and damned if we don't," like we can't ever do anything right. We insist we are doing the best we can and feel lost when we try to imagine what else we could be doing.

Many whites don't seem to know what more they can do. I can relate. I have often felt exasperated and thought, "What else do they want from me?" I desperately wanted someone to tell me what I should do because I had hit the edge of my competence and had absolutely no clue how to move forward. It took me years of floundering in this space before I could come from a place of humility and willingness to acknowledge and explore the depth of the racist beliefs and attitudes I struggle with. And I may never have made any meaningful progress except for the transformative growth I experience each time I co-facilitate another Social Justice Training Institute (SJTI).

Right after the experience at the Development Lab, some friends and I created SJTI as a way to give others a place to deepen their capacity as social justice educators. We wanted to give back to the field that had nurtured us. At that time, I had no idea how much I would grow and change in the process. In these very intense 5-day institutes, we focus on race and racism as a way to help participants expand their ability to dismantle oppression and create inclusive organizations. In each of the 36 SJTIs over the past 18 years, I have been challenged to take an increasingly honest look at myself, own my racist attitudes and behaviors, and then show up more authentically as a white change agent.

The most significant work for me occurs in the series of white caucuses I facilitate. It has been a gift to sit in these sacred spaces and support other whites as we face our fears and admit the racist attitudes and actions we commit in our organizations and in our daily lives. I am overwhelmed each SJTI at the sense of relief and hope white people feel as we realize we are not alone and that together we can find a way forward to partner with people of color to create greater racial justice. This journey is often not easy, but the results are miraculous at times.

I wrote this book to support other white people who are committed to social justice but find themselves feeling stuck and scared at times. I wrote this for those who spin in obsessive thoughts when they are called racist and who are beginning to hear that whisper in those early morning hours when they can't go back to sleep, that voice that wonders, "Maybe I'm not as good as I think I am. Maybe I am racist." My hope is that you will see yourself in my stories and my struggles as you discover new, more effective ways to be a white change agent. Mostly, I hope you realize you are not alone, and that there is a way to live with greater wholeness and integrity.

I can understand why some white people might quickly drop this book like a hot potato. This has been a hard, painful, and sometimes lonely journey. I have had to re-examine most everything I was ever taught or ever believed. I have had to face the truth about the impact of my racist actions and live with the knowledge that I can never undo the harm I have caused. But the pain of staying stuck and fearful was too great to bear. Once I began to wake up, I couldn't stand seeing the look of disappointment and anger on the faces of my colleagues of color when I once again said or did something racist. I wanted to be different. I could no longer live with myself knowing my actions perpetuated the racism that I said I was committed to eradicating.

It has been a long road and I am not done with this journey, but I do see some progress. I wrote this book to share much of what I know today in hopes that your journey on this path will be smoother and much faster than mine has been. The processes and tools in this book have supported my development over the years and reflect those I use at SJTI and share with coaching clients and workshop participants.

I hope you give yourself the gift of deep honesty as you read about the common fears and feelings of white allies as well as our predictable defenses when we are confronted on our racist behaviors. I hope you begin to recognize more of how you were socialized to be white and how you learned to believe racist stereotypes about people of color.

As you read about racist microaggressions and white privilege, I hope you choose to move through any debilitating guilt and shame you feel and realize the many ways you can effectively show up as a white change agent to shift racist interactions as well as dynamics of institutional racism. Most important, I hope you find the courage and compassion to participate in a community of white allies to continually do your self-work and develop deeper capacity to partner with people of color to create meaningful, sustainable change.

Today, I am far more likely to stay engaged as people of color name the racist attitudes and behaviors they experience from me. Don't get me wrong, I am still nervous and scared, but I can now stay in relationship to explore the impact of my behavior and commit to doing better in the future. I trust that those who confront me are giving me a chance to learn how to be more of the person I say I want to be. Being called racist isn't the end of the world; in fact, it can be a powerful opportunity to learn more about yourself and a gift to help you learn how to live your values each and every day.

It is a constant daily practice in willingness and humility. We need to learn from these experiences so we can become effective change agents for racial justice. We can shift the insidious, sometimes unconscious, racist beliefs that give us a false sense of superiority and entitlement as well as separate us from others and from our own humanity.

And some days, we will be better allies than others. But if we stay on the journey, we will make meaningful progress over time. I hope you make this commitment and join the millions of whites on whose shoulders we stand and who choose courage every day to live on purpose.

CHAPTER 1
I MEAN, I CAN'T BE RACIST!

A white client I'll call Patricia told me about a time a colleague of color pointed out her behavior that he experienced as racist:

When Jason confronted me after a meeting, I just froze and shut down. He was very upset that I had interrupted him to answer a question from another colleague who didn't seem to understand Jason's point. I was just trying to help. What had I done wrong? Why was he so mad at me? He said what I had done was racist. I can't be a racist! When I tried to explain why I did that, Jason just shook his head and said he needed to get back to work. As he walked away I got really nervous. What if he told others about this? What would people think of me? How would this hurt my reputation? Would his version of this moment become frozen in time and be the only thing people of color would think about me? And I still didn't know what I did that was so horrible. Much of that afternoon and evening I kept swirling in fear and disbelief. I just kept replaying that moment over and over, desperately trying to figure out what I had done so I could go back and get him to realize I wasn't as bad as he thought.

I wonder if you relate to Patricia and many whites I have met who waste so much time and life energy in fear that someone will call us racist. We become so over-focused with maintaining our reputation and trying to control what people of color think of us that we don't really listen to anyone's feedback, much less stay open to changing our behavior. When confronted by people of color, it is common for whites to freeze and spin out of control in fear and anxiety. At other times, we may feel incensed they had the audacity to criticize us in the first place.

I remember a time I was confronted by a colleague of color, and I was so irritated that she had pointed out such a small thing. I remember thinking, "How can you focus on this, when I have done so many good things as a white person and helped you out so many times? Haven't I earned some grace and credit?" Ah, no. The irony is, she probably wouldn't have even bothered to take the risk to talk to me if I hadn't shown up enough as a white ally for her to invest the time and energy. When she confronted me, I became defensive. I quickly interrupted and said, "That wasn't my intent! I was talking about...." As if repeating what I had said and dismissing the impact of my comment on her was at all useful in the moment. I kept arguing back and forth saying, "That's not what I said" a few times. And all the while thinking, "She is blowing this out of proportion."

I wonder if you can relate to ever using this tactic to avoid accepting responsibility for the impact of your behavior? Or like I also did, have you used a perfectly logical explanation to dismiss this type of feedback?

There are many other ways white people react unproductively when people of color try to give us feedback about our behaviors. Have you ever argued that people of color misunderstood what you said? Or that this was just an isolated incident, and you were just triggered and misspoke in the heat of the moment? Or have you tried to explain away your actions by claiming your comment actually had nothing to do with race? Or have you started credentialing and saying how your good friend, who happens to be black, uses that same phrase, so what is the big deal? Have you tried to defend what you did by pointing out how it was not as bad as what other whites have been saying? Or insisted, "At least I'm trying! Why aren't you confronting the others in the office?"

I have thought or done all of these. I know I have felt I am damned if I do and damned if I don't, believing that if I speak up, I get confronted and misunderstood, but if I am quiet, then people of color are mad at me for not showing up. I've thought, "I can't ever get it right, so why bother?" And as a result, I have given up trying–meaning I have sat back and stayed silent, not realizing how this is another example of using my white privilege to drop out and not take the risk to pay attention and respond to racist dynamics in the workplace.

Another way white people try to dodge any responsibility is by accusing people of color of playing the race card or being overly sensitive or too aggressive in their reactions. A Latino workshop participant I'll call Julian told me an example of this dynamic. In a team meeting, his manager, who is white, made a racist joke, and several team members laughed along. When Julian said he didn't appreciate the comment, his manager looked furious, changed the subject, and started talking about the next item on the agenda. After the meeting, Julian got a call from the manager's administrative assistant to come meet with the manager. As he walked into the office, his manager immediately said Julian's comment was unprofessional and inappropriate, and he should never again attack him like that in public.

I can relate to how the manager reacted. Sometimes when people of color name our behavior as offensive, whites will critique how the feedback was given to us and focus on their timing, tone, or phrasing instead of listening, acknowledging, and exploring the impact of our comments. We shift the focus off of our behavior by insisting the person of color didn't give us feedback in an appropriate manner. Without coaching, many whites may never realize how we are not only dismissing the voices and input of people of color but are also using tone policing to enforce some of the white cultural rules about what is correct, supposedly professional, behavior.

All of these defense mechanisms are attempts to shift the focus away from the impact of our comments to avoid examining our implicit racial bias, our racist attitudes, and the resulting impact of our behavior. We are trying to hold on to the illusion we are a "good white" and by defending ourselves, we are only replicating racist dynamics and reinforcing the reality that we are not as competent as we think we are. In the process, we once again re-center whiteness, meaning we only talk about our own issues and concerns and those of other whites, without giving any credence or attention to what people of color are trying to tell us.

After being confronted, it is common for white people to shut down and withdraw from any further conversation. We may say we are giving people of color space to talk when in reality we are punishing them with the silent treatment for having the audacity to take us on. And even this thought of giving them space reflects the white supremacist belief that whites own time and space, and it is ours to allocate and use as we see fit.

Another unproductive way white people react is staying stuck in white guilt. We often trap ourselves in our feelings of guilt and shame by replaying negative, self-condemning thoughts and judgments over and over in our minds. These are some common ones I often hear from whites: I'm such a fraud; I'm a horrible white ally; I can't do anything right; I am so incompetent; How could I have done something so racist? Did I just ruin this relationship? What if I say something else racist? I am such a bad person!

We become entangled in these unproductive thoughts, beating ourselves up instead of learning from our missteps and continuing to move forward. Now don't get me wrong. I believe a little guilt keeps us humble enough to be willing to recognize the impact of our behaviors, make amends, and change our actions in the future. However, I have also used deep guilt and shame to justify why I am sitting on the sidelines, wallowing in self-pity and fear, and not taking the risk to show up authentically in the moment.

Shame, in my opinion, is rarely if ever useful. When I am feeling ashamed, I feel like I am bad and defective as a person, and I hardly ever see a way out of this seemingly bottomless pit. Shame is rooted in dualistic white cultural beliefs that everything is good or bad, right or wrong. You are either a good person or a bad person, a good white ally or a bad one. There is no in-between. When I am deep in shame, I am focused on my essence as a person, feeling helpless and hopeless, believing that I can never change and be different. But, if instead, I feel guilty about the impact of what I've said or done, I can use these emotions to motivate me to focus on how to change my racist attitudes and behaviors.

A client told me how she had used the terms "illegal aliens" and "illegal immigrants" in a meeting and how afterwards a colleague of color had spoken to her about using those racist terms. She was shocked and quickly asked how she should say it right. When her colleague said, "It's not my job to educate you," she felt upset and helpless.

This is a common dynamic. When we are confronted about our comments or actions, whites may start to obsess and try to figure out exactly what NOT to say or do in the future in an attempt to prevent ever getting negative feedback again. We ask people of color to teach us how we should say things "right" the next time without realizing the tremendous burden we put on our colleagues to constantly educate us. We selfishly focus on how not to be called out again, instead of working to understand what happened and take responsibility for identifying and changing the racist attitudes that fueled our behavior.

Can you imagine how we would be different if instead we chose to embrace the moment and humbly, honestly, and authentically engage people of color? The times that I have been able to stay present in these moments are when I have framed the situation not as an attack but as an opportunity to learn more about myself and possibly see how I need to shift my actions to better align with my core values. When I have appreciated people of color for taking the risk to give me feedback, I have been more willing and open to listen deeply, look at my part in the interaction, and commit to changing my behavior so I do less harm in the future.

But more often than not, if you are like me, we feel so deeply triggered when confronted by people of color that we do not respond effectively. We swirl in a range of feelings, including embarrassment, anxiety, guilt, and shame. We may feel surprised, caught off-guard, confused, and unsure about what we have done, much less what to do next. We may quickly regret the impact of our comments and feel remorseful, while at other times we may feel overwhelmed, deflated, discouraged, or disheartened and believe we may never be a good enough ally.

These common emotional reactions may be fueled by numerous fears that were retriggered in the moment. Over the years I have collected numerous examples of fears from people in the white caucuses I have facilitated. My guess is you can relate to feeling some of these, including: What if I make a mistake or say something racist? Will people see me as incompetent? Will this hurt my relationships with people of color? Will it hurt my reputation? Will I lose credibility? Is this a career-ending move? Will this moment come to define me so people always think of me as racist? What if they think I am a fraud? Will people be disappointed in me or feel I've let them down? What if people get hurt or I make things worse? What if I never get it right? Or what if what I do really doesn't make any difference? These fears are debilitating. When I am swirling in these fears, I am triggered and not present enough to engage effectively.

In addition to these fears, our ego often gets in our way. Our wanting to be seen as competent, to be in control, and to be right may show up in unproductive thoughts, including: No one appreciates all that I do! They should know I would never do anything on purpose! No one has ever raised this as a problem before. They just don't like me and are making a big deal out of nothing. I would never do something racist! These thoughts are examples of how our judgments of others create barriers and obstacles we trip over as we try to respond to the feedback from both people of color and other white allies.

There is another defensive reaction that undermines our efforts as change agents: white women's tears. I have heard many people of color feel deeply frustrated when whites, particularly white women, start to cry when confronted about their behavior. The predictable pattern is that all of the attention quickly gets redirected off of the racist dynamic and focused onto taking care of the white woman while disparaging the person of color for being too aggressive or mean. I have observed these common group dynamics throughout my career and watched how the conversation is rarely refocused back to the original issues that were problematic. No one wins in these situations; white women and other whites in the room do not learn enough to change their attitudes and behaviors, the concerns of people of color are once again ignored and pushed to the side, and the person who raised the issue may now also be erroneously burdened with the racist labels of "difficult to work with" or a "trouble-maker."

There is another way to respond in these moments. When a white woman starts to cry, I ask her to take some deep breaths as I invite the group to let her experience her feelings and not try to take care of her or rescue her in the moment. I clearly state that this person can easily be in her feelings and continue engaging and doesn't need to be comforted or saved by anyone. I then refocus my attention onto the white woman and say how I really respect people who can express their emotions and talk through their tears. I then ask if she is ready to share her reactions to the feedback. In the vast majority of situations, white women are able to continue engaging effectively, and group members realize a number of things, including: people can cry and talk at the same time; jumping in to support someone may be more about trying to avoid our own feelings of discomfort; interrupting the learning moment by handing out Kleenex, rubbing someone's back or challenging the person of color's comments may deny the white woman a potentially important growth opportunity; and the entire group may benefit from fully experiencing and processing this emotional moment.

All of these defensive behaviors, feelings, fears, and unproductive thoughts keep us stuck and ineffective as white allies. We either stay silent or react in ways that perpetuate and reinforce racist dynamics. The ways we react out of our deep fear of being called racist undermines our core values and vision of ourselves as an effective change agent.

There is another way. The first step is to recognize and own our fears and defensive reactions. The next step is to be willing to accept responsibility to change ourselves, even if we don't yet know how.

CHAPTER 2
BECOMING AWARE
OF OUR RACIST
COMMENTS

I think the first time I was asked to think about my race journey and socialization experiences was in a doctoral course with Dr. Bailey Jackson when he asked questions like, "When was the first time you realized you were white?" and "What were ways that whites were treated compared to people of color?" Until then, I had been learning about race and racism by reading about the horrible life experiences of people of color but never had considered how whiteness, white supremacy, and white privilege impacted me or how I, as a white person, perpetuated systems of oppression. All that would come later. In this class I began to reflect on my life experiences. I invite you to see how you might relate to these aspects of my story and how your journey was different.

I grew up in the 1960's in a white, middle/professional class suburb about 10 miles outside of Washington, D.C. All of my neighbors were white families; I only played with other white children and walked to my elementary school where all my teachers and principals were white. I remember there were once two black students in my 3rd or 4th grade class.

I remember their first names to this day, though doubt I ever knew their last names. I never invited either of them to play or to a birthday party, as I did some white friends in my class. I never wondered what it was like for them to walk home in the opposite direction from me, literally across the railroad tracks to where they lived. I do remember my mom driving us across those tracks many times through that part of town and always saying, "Lock your doors." I never questioned her or asked why.

The only other person of color I remember meeting was the black woman who was a maid in a friend's house a couple doors down, whose name I don't remember or never knew. No person of color ever came to our house. But I learned a lot about race from all the images of people of color and whites I saw on all the TV shows and movies I watched as a kid. I loved watching The Lone Ranger and other Western-themed shows. I had no idea at the time how I was absorbing racist messages about Native Americans, Mexican Americans, and people of mixed race heritage from these shows. I never questioned or consciously noticed how all the heroes and leaders were white or how the villains were always people of color or white people who wore black hats and clothing. Additionally, I believe I saw every war movie ever made. What was I learning as I watched the portrayals of white US soldiers fighting the Japanese in WWII or white Union soldiers fighting and dying to end slavery?

These same messages of white superiority and righteousness were replicated in every history lesson or library book I read about "our country's heroes." I learned that whites brought civilization to this land and the nations on other continents. I never noticed how white people were always portrayed as "civilizing" and bringing Christianity to people of color. I just accepted and believed what I was taught. Everywhere I turned I saw whites in leadership and professional roles as principals, teachers, police officers, presidents, doctors, coaches, supervisors, and ministers, Girl Scout leaders, and camp counselors. I don't remember personally meeting any person of color in any leadership or positive role in my life until my doctoral program.

I was a young girl in the mid-60s as I watched the evening news and saw horrific images of the KKK and white police officers brutalizing Civil Rights marchers and protesters. Even as a young child I believed this was wrong. I was eleven when Dr. King was assassinated, and I remember being in a car with my mom passing by Resurrection City and feeling fear as we drove through areas of D.C. with burned-out row houses. From someone or somewhere I had been told that "the blacks had rioted" after Dr. King was killed, and they had "destroyed their own neighborhoods." When Mom told me to lock the doors, I readily did and felt such relief when I saw a military truck pass by with white National Guard soldiers carrying weapons. No one offered me another way to make meaning of what I was seeing. I never remember talking directly about race in my home or discussing what I saw on TV. No one challenged me to question the racist messages I had accepted through-out my youth.

My county and our local school system were desegregated in 1970. I was about to start 9th grade at that time, and I remember my classmates and I were to be bussed to an all-black junior high. I remember my parents talking around me that they didn't want me to go to that school because I was smart and they wanted me to get a good education. They arranged for me and other siblings to attend a private, religiously-affiliated high school that was all white. At the time, and for decades afterwards, I never recognized or questioned their racially coded language and rationale. I was a good student and wanted to excel, and I readily fol-lowed the path they chose for me. In 1991, I actually met a black man who attended that junior high school, and we quickly realized we would have been in the same grade. As we talked and got to know each other a bit, I couldn't help but wonder who I might have become if I had not been a part of the white flight in 1970. How might I have been different from having all those opportunities to learn from, learn with, and play sports with people of color in those early years? How might my perceptions of the world have been changed if I had spent my teens in a more racially diverse environment? I might possibly have developed key cultural competencies while unlearning racist stereotypes.

I was a history major in college and focused on the Civil War in my senior thesis. I examined what I believed to be the real motives of President Lincoln to use the Emancipation

Proclamation to save the Union, not to end slavery, as was the common belief. As a student teacher in high school history classes, I taught what and how I had been schooled, without any racial or social justice consciousness at all. I have few memories of that semester in that classroom, but I do remember this one 10th grade class and how several black young men all sat one behind each other in a row against the window. They never seemed to be engaged or learning what I was teaching, so I left them alone. I never tried to get to know them or explore how they were feeling in the class. Their behavior mirrored what I had been socialized to expect from black students, and I never questioned the racist bias fueling my assumptions and actions.

I never thought about my family as having any prejudices, mostly because I never recognized that I had any. I remember being in an education class the first semester of my Master's program and fighting with the young instructor. He was asking us to examine how our values and biases impact how we teach, and I vehemently argued that as a student teacher I taught without my values or beliefs impacting me at all! I quickly dropped that class.

In spite of my resistance and lack of awareness or questioning, somewhere I must have begun to shift a bit because I remember coming home when I was a graduate student for the December break and was shocked that my mother had started telling racist jokes and making racist comments! My guess is that in reality I had just begun to notice what may have been around me throughout my early years.

I share these stories to give some context and background for where I have come from and what has helped shape me. I wish I could start telling stories of how I soon became a conscientious advocate for racial justice, but that wouldn't happen for a couple more decades. I grew up in a cocoon of whiteness, white culture, and white supremacy and never questioned or challenged it. In my first couple of work environments, I had a few opportunities to work with people of color but I never developed any type of connection or relationship with them. I continued to judge their comments, their behaviors, and their capacity as less than mine, less than whites, without ever questioning how my racist socialization had me believe I was smarter and better as a white person.

I don't remember ever saying or doing anything overtly racist. I never used derogatory terms or expressed racist ideology. However, I now realize that I didn't have to be blatant in my actions to still reinforce racism through my racist attitudes and behaviors. My actions were fueled by beliefs that whites were smarter and superior to people of color and that we deserved everything in our lives because we had worked hard and earned it.

While I have told some of these stories in trainings and coaching sessions, this is the first time I have written them down all together. As I reread them, I feel a sick heaviness as I realize so many ways I perpetuated and reinforced racist dynamics and worked to maintain the status quo of my white privilege through my racist attitudes and behaviors.

I worked to keep this illusion of superiority intact at the expense of the people of color in my life. And I modeled and taught ways of leading, training, and engaging that reinforced racism in the workplace and in society.

I never had any role models to show me another way for the first three decades of my life. And I never went outside the box to learn on my own. In turn, as a leader and an educator, I taught other whites the same racist attitudes and actions and, in the process, privileged and advantaged whites as I continued to disadvantage and oppress people of color. A hard reality for me to face and own, yet it is the truth.

"Sometimes people don't want to hear the truth because they don't want their illusions destroyed."
Friedrich Nietzsche

I began to have a few experiences that whispered a different way to be. In the mid-1980's I supervised a white male graduate student who told me he was thinking about doing a practicum in the Black Student Services office. I remember feeling shocked and asking something like, "Why would you do that?" Several years later, he invited my partner and me to go with him to a weeklong seminar at The Martin Luther King, Jr. Center for Nonviolent Social Change in Atlanta. It was an amazing week of learning from some of the key leaders of the Civil Rights Movement and the first time I remember seeing whites actively talking about racial justice.

A few years later my white partner came home from one of the many seminars and classes on race and racism that she was experiencing in her workplace. I remember her talking on and on about white privilege and whiteness; I had no clue what she was talking about and dismissed her enthusiasm as naïve. I was focused on my workshops on sexism and homophobia with no consciousness of how I was training only out of my subordinated identities and approaching these topics from a white, female, and lesbian frame of reference. I was really only trying to create more acceptance and inclusion for myself and those who were like me.

Then I took classes with Dr. Bailey Jackson and other faculty at the University of Massachusetts at Amherst who challenged me to move beyond "diversity" to begin to understand the dynamics of oppression and the role that members of the dominant or privileged group play in colluding with and perpetuating systems of racism and other forms of oppression. I learned far more knowledge about the history of race and racism and began to develop a bit more of a critical race lens. Possibly the most significant impact in my race journey was having my first personal relationship with a person of color who so graciously invested time and energy into my growth and development. I began to care about issues of race and racism differently because now they were negatively impacting people I cared about.

My life changed significantly when I was invited to join a consulting group owned by an African American woman, Elsie Y. Cross. The goal of her work was to facilitate transformative culture change in organizations and ameliorate oppression. One of the major interventions was a 5-day workshop that directly addressed issues of sexism and racism in organizations. Most significantly for me, the way the training staff worked together gave me consistent opportunities to grow and change, ones I rarely appreciated at the time.

As we met to plan the sessions, we always reflected on how we were engaging across race and gender and gave each other clear, direct feedback in the process. Those conversations were often raw and deeply conflictual. I often resisted the feedback but my colleagues were persistent and cared enough about me not to let me off the hook. I learned to follow the leadership of people of color and to recognize and appreciate their skills, wisdom, and talent. These experiences began to shatter the white supremacist beliefs I held onto that whites were smarter and better, superior to people of color. I wish I could say I was a fast learner and that I changed quickly, but this is not the case. I am deeply grateful to the many colleagues I had the privilege to work with who consistently, with love and grace, patiently worked with me and helped me begin to challenge and change deeply rooted racist attitudes and behaviors.

Additionally, I can't over-emphasize the critical role that white colleagues had in modeling for me more effective ways to be a white change agent. For the first time, I saw whites use their "self as instrument" and tell stories of times they acted out of racist attitudes and relate with compassion as other whites authentically shared about their own racist socialization and behaviors. At the same time, they also confronted the racial prejudice and racist behaviors of white participants and staff.

I thought I was doing well with this group of trainers until one of my white mentors sat me down one evening for a more in-depth evaluation of my performance to date. By then the consulting firm was also addressing issues of heterosexism in the workshops, and so she gave me a visual representation of her assessment of my competence. She raised one hand above her head and said, "This is where I have your competence around heterosexism, very high." Then she brought her hand down to about her head and said, "And this is where I see your capacity around sexism." And then she bent down and put her hand about a foot above the floor and said, "And this is where I see you in your competence as a white person and racism." No one had ever so directly given me that degree of honest feedback, or at least I had never heard it before. And while I resisted in the moment, I soon accepted that she was right and committed myself to doing more, doing better. This probably occurred in 1997 or 1998, soon after that disastrous experience in the Development Lab I talked about in the Introduction. Looking back, those experiences were the best thing that could have happened to me, though at the time I was shaken to my core.

My experiences with the leaders and colleagues in Elsie Y. Cross Associates changed my life, my life path. All that I learned with them was instrumental in shaping my contributions to how we designed the Social Justice Training Institute. Their legacy lives on through our pedagogy, much of the content, and, particularly, how I facilitate the white caucuses.

While I didn't start out this way in 1999 at our first SJTI race immersion, today I believe I engage other whites with deep compassion and care as I rigorously confront their racist attitudes and behaviors. As I tell my own stories and recent examples of acting out of racist beliefs, I invite them to relate and connect with my stories. I believe we create a learning environment within which whites can honestly look in the mirror, and without debilitating guilt and shame, authentically acknowledge their racist behaviors and attitudes as they make a renewed, deeply passionate choice to begin again and heal from their racist socialization. Together, we commit at a very deep level to deepen our capacity as white change agents to truly partner with and follow the leadership of people of color to dismantle racism.

I am at my best at SJTI, surrounded by amazing colleagues and friends, as we design and facilitate significant, transformative learning for so many. I just wish I always showed up as authentic and competent in the rest of my life. I am on this journey and some days I am awake and creating liberation for myself and with others, and other days I can forget I am white.

I still have moments where I freeze and do not confront racist comments for fear of hurting a relationship or the chance of being hired. And in the process, I throw people of color under the bus to keep my privileged status. I sometimes still get defensive and resist the feedback from people of color or other whites who are only trying to help me be the person I say I want to be. And I can still feel triggered and become overly aggressive as I confront other whites on their comments and actions. As a result, I miss the opportunity to build a bridge and facilitate learning and growth. The good news is, I usually recognize what I am doing sooner than I used to, and most often, I come back to apologize, make amends, and commit to do better the next time. I am in this for the long haul, and I hope you are, too. To borrow some key 12 Step concepts, this journey is about progress, not perfection, doing better one day at a time.

As the Rev. Dr. Jamie Washington reminds us with one of his *Diverse Community Foundations*, "It is not our fault, but we must accept responsibility." I couldn't control how I was socialized or what racist beliefs I unconsciously absorbed in my youth. It is not our fault that we learned and believed the underlying racist messages that permeate our society, but we now must take responsibility for what we learned, honestly own and interrogate all that we were taught, and then commit to a daily practice of eradicating these racist beliefs and actions from our lives.

We can't get there from here unless we act on this deep commitment to change. Just like we spot weeds in a garden, every single day we must be vigilant and persistent to recognize the slightest whisper of a racist thought, the more subtle actions that perpetuate whiteness and white supremacy and then interrupt our racist thoughts and behaviors every moment of every day. This is a significant part of what it means to be a white ally, in my opinion. Every moment we have a choice to either collude and perpetuate racism or speak up and create liberation. Which will you choose? The challenge is, many times we feel deeply committed, but don't know what to do or how to change.

CHAPTER 3
RECOGNIZING RACIST COMMENTS AND ACTIONS: TOOLS TO RESPOND

A multiracial workshop participant I'll call Gabriela told me about a challenging search committee meeting where she felt completely invisible and dismissed.

We were under pressure to finalize the list of candidates we were going to invite to campus for the next round of interviews. All of the candidates discussed so far had been white. I tried to expand the conversation by recommending my top candidate, a man of color with an exceptional resume, in my opinion. As I was about to explain why he was my top pick, a white committee member interrupted me and said, "I don't think Roberto has the background we are looking for." I continued by saying, "It's Gilberto, and if we look back at the stated criteria for the position, he clearly has the depth of experience and demonstrated competence we are seeking." The chair, a white woman, then said, "I did like what he said, but I had trouble understanding him at times." I then said how I had no trouble understanding his points and no one asked him any clarifying questions in the interview. As I was about to continue, the chair turned away from me and asked another white colleague who their top 3 picks were. I tried to come back into the conversation, but the chair said we didn't have much more time and we needed to hear from everyone else. It seemed only a short moment before the chair was summarizing the group's supposed consensus, which did not include Gilberto. I quickly jumped in and said that I think all three of these possible finalists were white and again advocated for Gilberto. I looked at a white friend of mine to see if they would back me up. They just silently looked back at me. Then the person who had earlier misnamed Gilberto said, "We had a diverse pool, and now we need to choose the most qualified candidates." I looked back at my white friend, who once again didn't speak up. I felt so exhausted and depleted.

After the meeting, I tried to talk with the chair, but she was running to teach a class. I checked in with my friend and asked why he hadn't spoken up. All he said was that Gilberto wasn't in his top 3 list. When I confronted him about not intervening to interrupt the many racist microaggressions in that meeting, he looked a little shocked and asked me what had happened from my perspective. At that point I just told him I had a meeting I needed to attend.

I can relate to her white friend. I have missed noticing, much less interrupting, so many racist microaggressions over the years. I have consistently under-estimated the cumulative negative impact of these seemingly minor moments on my colleagues of color. I have been so overly focused on completing assignments and being on time, core white cultural norms, that I have often overlooked the common racist dynamics that occurred around me as I was focused on the task, not our process.

It is critical we sharpen our awareness of the common types of racist comments and actions so we quickly recognize and shift these microaggressions in the moment. In this chapter I first highlight some common racist dynamics and the internalized attitudes and beliefs that fuel them. I then offer specific strategies to respond effectively to create greater racial justice.

Examples of Racist Microaggressions

See if you can relate to having done any of the following microaggressions that I no doubt have committed in my life. Too often, it is easy to overlook these subtle daily indignities and only confront the very blatant racist comments. As you review these, you may want to note the underlying racial prejudice and white supremacist attitudes that are under most of these, such as that white people are smarter, better, and superior to people of color; or whites deserve the benefit of the doubt and to be assumed competent from the start, etc. If you start to feel resistance as you read the following examples or think, "That happens to whites, too," it may be helpful to consider how often it happens to white people compared to the frequency with which people of color experience these microaggressions.

In my experience whites tend to interrupt and talk over people of color or rephrase what they have just said. I remember doing this and believing I was helping because I thought I could say it in ways that would be better understood by others. We tend to be far more critical and questioning of the comments and suggestions from people of color and expect them to prove themselves as competent, instead of assuming they are competent from the start. I have seen white people argue more forcefully with people of color and insist, and believe, they were right and the folks of color were wrong. This dynamic is significantly different from what I observe as whites disagree with other white people.

If we can increase our awareness of these subtle, and not so subtle, daily indignities, then we may be more prepared to respond effectively in the moment. Here are some more examples. I have seen white people enthusiastically greet each other before a meeting as they ignore the person of color in the room or greet them more impersonally. It is common for whites to listen intently as other white people speak, yet give far less respect when people of color offer ideas as we check our phones, have side conversations, or dismiss their idea, until a few minutes later, as a white colleague mentions a very similar thought, we accept it as a great idea. I have been in meetings where I was assumed to be the leader when it was my colleague of color who was in charge. I have been introduced as Dr. Kathy Obear when my colleague of color with a doctorate has been introduced as "Ms."

Another common racist dynamic I see occurs in trainings. I rarely, if ever, get questioned or challenged when I am co-facilitating with colleagues of color, especially if they identify as female. And yet predictably, almost every time, I watch participants ask my colleague to repeat instructions, challenge her statements and credentials, and often decide they don't need to follow her directions at all.

Other common microaggressions I have done are repeatedly mispronouncing a person of color's name and calling two people of color by each other's name when they look nothing alike. I have seen white allies who raise concerns about racist organizational dynamics be praised and valued for their input. Yet, when people of color bring up issues, they may be ignored or experience resistance as well as exclusion from the many informal interactions and social activities where employees often receive support, coaching, and opportunities to develop productive working relationships. I have even seen the pattern of white supervisors raising their voice to end conversations and shut down people of color who are trying to share feedback or concerns.

A particularly painful comment I made when I saw several people of color talking in a small group was, "I hope you are not up to any trouble!" When confronted about this, my first reaction was, "Oh, I was only joking," when in reality, I have never said anything close to this to the many small groups of white employees I see talking among themselves every day in organizations. This is another example of how many whites may feel nervous and more uncomfortable talking to people of color, and so we walk on eggshells or use inappropriate jokes to try to connect.

In her book *Promoting Diversity and Social Justice*, Dr. Diane J. Goodman talks about other actions that white people do that create barriers to working collaboratively across race including when we demand things be done in ways that reflect white cultural norms. As a result, whites often take over or insert themselves into projects or conversations because we think we know more and can do it more efficiently.

Another frustrating microaggression is how whites rarely value the input and contributions of people of color, and yet we expect them to help the organization appear more diverse by being visible and active on many more task forces and search committees than ever expected of white members of the organization. In addition, we expect our colleagues of color to readily allow their pictures to be displayed on organizational websites and other marketing materials. They are also expected to drop whatever they are doing to handle situations involving issues of race when white colleagues feel uncomfortable or realize, though never admit, they don't know what to do. It is also ironic how many white people think we are superior to people of color, and yet we expect and demand they teach us about issues of racism and diversity as well as expect them to applaud us and give us praise for our efforts to create racial justice.

I could keep going, but one final pattern that clearly undermines our effectiveness is how we take up significant time and energy in discussions compared to that of people of color. Our actions have negative impact whether we are interrupting to explain our intent or to argue our point, or when we defensively criticize people of color for attacking us when they were merely disagreeing, or when, in a patronizing or condescending manner, whites try to teach people of color about racism, sometimes referred to as "whitesplaining." In all of these moments, we are re-centering ourselves and our issues, re-centering whiteness, and minimizing and dismissing the concerns and issues of people of color.

Recognizing when we do these racist actions can be challenging. In the times I have wanted to resist acknowledging my own patterns of behavior, it has been helpful to ask myself, "Do I treat everyone this way? Or do I tend to treat whites differently from people of color? Would I ever do to a white person what I just did to a person of color?" In reality, it can be hard to reflect on our own patterns, so it may be useful to ask a couple other white colleagues to track your interactions over a week and then give you feedback and coaching. While this may initially feel scary to do, I can attest to the significant value of having a small group of trusted whites give me honest, relevant feedback to help me be a more effective change agent.

Exploring Internalized Dominance

I hope you have honestly reflected on your own behaviors as you read the first part of this chapter. A key step for me to take responsibility for my actions has been to identify and critically examine the attitudes and beliefs I hold that fuel many of these racist behaviors. It is very common for white people who grew up in the U.S. culture to have absorbed, possibly unconsciously, many racist attitudes and beliefs. In the resources on my website, www.drkathyobear.com/racebook, I have posted a longer list of these common racist dynamics that are so prevalent in our society and fuel many racist comments and reactions of whites. In addition, I have posted a list of definitions and terms that may be useful.

The following are examples of internalized dominance, racist beliefs that white people have adopted, often unconsciously, that support the idea that white people are better than people of color (Bell, et. al., 2016). Internalized dominance also refers to actions of white people, based on a racist belief system of superiority, that perpetuate and maintain racism in organizations and society. These racist beliefs include believing people of color are not as competent and are hired only because of their race and Affirmative Action quotas. There are several additional beliefs related to this one: 1) that white people are smarter and more competent than people of color; 2) that everything whites have accomplished is because we worked hard and "earned it," rather than being the beneficiaries of a vast system of white privilege; and 3) that people of color are to blame for the hardships they experience. Many whites believe that if people of color would only work harder, they could pull themselves up by their bootstraps and succeed as easily as whites. I appreciated a comment I once heard from a person of color, "We never had boots in the first place! Whites took those, too!"

Another example of internalized dominance includes believing that white cultural norms and practices are superior to those of other cultures and, as a result, people of color should conform and assimilate without challenge or question. These attitudes and white cultural dynamics are so pervasive and insidious that the vast majority of whites have never even considered there are other possible ways to create effective, productive work environments. I didn't even begin to understand or question white culture until relatively recently. I could recognize and interrupt micro-aggressions but hadn't seriously explored the dynamics of whiteness, white supremacy, and institutional racism in organizations. I explore these concepts in more detail in a later chapter.

In white caucuses I facilitate, participants readily discuss additional examples of internalized dominance they experience. For example, we often resent taking direction from a leader of color and feel safer around people of color who have assimilated and model white cultural norms. Because we believe organizations and white cultural practices are good and fair, many of us tend to dismiss and minimize frustrations of people of color as complaints by employees that "have a bad attitude" or who aren't a "team player". We feel defensive when people of color raise issues and want them to "just get over it" so we can all move on. In addition, if there is possibly one situation that we think could have involved race dynamics, we are quick to rationalize it away as an isolated incident and a misunderstanding because we insist that the white person who did something inappropriate is a good person and would never do something like that. This type of rationalization is grounded in the positive bias that whites are good-hearted people who would never intentionally do anything harmful.

Most of the time when people of color raise issues we judge them as over-reacting, being too sensitive, and playing the race card. One root of this is our white cultural belief in individualism and the subsequent mindset that everything that happens to people is a result of their own individual actions: If something bad happened to a person of color, it was probably because of something they did or didn't do. Most whites do not yet have the willingness or capacity to acknowledge the cumulative impact of the years, decades, and centuries of racism that people of color experience. We rationalize away any incident by blaming the victim, refusing to consider the pervasive impact of institutional racism. All of these examples of internalized dominance work to keep the status quo of white privilege and institutional racism in place in organizations.

While most of us haven't intentionally decided to believe or act on racist assumptions and implicit biases, our behaviors, whether we are conscious of this or not, support and perpetuate racism in our organizations. I believe it takes courage to honestly admit we have these racist attitudes and internalized beliefs, and it is critical that we each take responsibility for eliminating all of them from our psyche. It may take even more courage to do the depth of essential self-work to heal from our racist socialization and training as we dig under our biases to honestly identify the reasons we hold onto these racist attitudes and the pay-off we receive from believing them. This is the only way I know to move out of guilt and into constructive action.

It is possible to live another way, and we must do our part, every single day, to accept responsibility for the impact of our racist attitudes and actions, and consistently choose to respond differently, in ways that create true racial justice. If we do not, we will continue to dehumanize people of color, and in the process, dehumanize ourselves.

Tools to Engage Others at the Interpersonal Level

Let me start with what NOT to do. There are a number of Dialogue Traps I learned as a consultant in Elsie Y. Cross Associates (EYCA) that are clearly unproductive and grounded in racist beliefs. Unfortunately, I have fallen into all of these traps throughout my life!

Intent vs. Impact

For instance, any time a white person is confronted about the impact of our behavior, our first response most likely is, "That wasn't my intent!" I relate to this predictable tendency to immediately justify our comment by focusing on our intent, as if this would minimize the impact of our actions. I often interrupt the other person and start to defend my intent to avoid being thought of as racist.

I am far more effective when I simply pause, breathe, apologize, and ask if the person would be willing to share more about the impact I had. The key at this point is to resist the urge to argue and debate by saying "Yea, but" in hopes of convincing the person of color they misunderstood me. Instead, I find it more useful to acknowledge what I heard to be the impact and commit to changing my behavior in the future.

Perfectly Logical Explanations (PLEs)

Another common trap is the Perfectly Logical Explanation or PLEs. So often, I have used a PLE to try to explain away, unsuccessfully, how a comment or action had nothing to do with race. For instance, if a person of color shares how someone said to him, "You are so articulate," a very intense trigger phrase, I have seen whites come back quickly saying, "I say that to everyone. It's a compliment." Or if a person of color confronts a white colleague for consistently interrupting her in a meeting, I have seen other white people try to rescue their colleague with a common PLE, "Oh, that has nothing to do with race. She is an affirmative action interrupter. She interrupts everyone. She interrupts me all the time!" Note both the added trigger of misusing the term "Affirmative Action" as well as another classic Dialogue Trap, "That happens to me, too!"

I know someone who...

Another way I have tried to defend myself when confronted about a racist comment is to use the Trap "I know someone who" by saying, "I have an Asian friend who uses that term, so it can't be racist!" Or I have tried to turn the tables by accusing the person of color of over-reacting and being too sensitive.

The exception, not the rule

A final trap that disrupts meaningful engagement and stifles potential learning is "That doesn't happen to me or friends of mine." For example, when people of color share how they were just racially profiled, pulled over, and aggressively confronted by a police officer in their predominantly white neighborhood, I have heard whites reply, "That has never happened to me or to any of my friends of color." A common next comment often results in blaming the victim. "Were you respectful to the officer? My black friends tell me they just smile and do whatever the police officer says, and they are treated as well as I am." All of these Dialogue Traps dismiss and discount the lived experiences of people of color, question their veracity and credibility, and deny the existence of racist dynamics.

Tools to Engage Effectively

Once I accepted the fact that I still believed racist attitudes and acted out of internalized dominance, I was far better situated to effectively engage other whites when I noticed their racist behaviors. Instead of calling white people out from a stance of self-righteous anger or from an ego-driven desire to be seen as the "good white," I am far more likely today to move into the conversation from a compassionate place because I recognize in myself what they have said or done. I no longer have to attack them in order to deny I have done the very same behaviors. I now have the tools and emotional clarity, on most days, to meet whites where they are, relate to them by letting them know I have had similar racist thoughts and made similar racist comments, and then offer them what I have learned over time and other ways to respond.

For instance, in a recent seminar on equity and inclusion, a white faculty member said something like, "I don't see color. I am color-blind." I sensed an energy shift in the room and responded by asking, "I'm curious what your intent was behind using the term, color-blind?' I have used that term in the past without realizing the impact on others. My guess is you know that is a trigger phrase for many people." When he nodded, I continued, "Tell me where I'm wrong, but my guess is as you look around this room, you recognize some people who may identify as Latinx, Asian American, African American, and maybe some who identify as Native American, Middle Eastern, Multiracial or Biracial." As he nodded again, I said, "So you see color, you recognize different racial identities. Can you say more about what you meant to communicate when you said you were color-blind?"

He then said he treated all people with the same respect, regardless of their race, and he didn't let the color of someone's skin impact what he thought about them or how he treated them. I acknowledged his comments and continued, "I join you in this vision of treating people of color with dignity and respect. Today, I think some people use the term color-blind in a different way to try to discount and minimize the common racist dynamics that exist, to try to convince others we are 'post racial.' I trust that wasn't your intent, though my guess is this was the impact you may have had on people just now." I paused and he said, "No, that was not my intent, but I can see your point." As I moved to refocus back on the rest of the participants, I said, "Over the years I have learned that I have to be vigilant about seeing color and recognizing racial differences so that I can notice negative differential treatment and do my part to interrupt all the daily microaggressions people of color experience in the workplace. I'm curious what others are thinking and feeling."

I had several intentions as I engaged this white participant. I wanted to help him see the impact of his comment while also knowing I related to using that term as well. I wanted him not to feel isolated or targeted by my comments but joined and engaged out of compassion. I also wanted to be clear about the possible unintended impact of his comment and to help him and possibly others understand the negative context of that phrase. Finally, I could have just invited others to respond to his comment from the start, but I hadn't seen many white people show up very effectively in the session, so I wanted to model how a white person can engage and confront another white person in ways that could further learning and understanding.

In this short interaction, I used five different types of skills that I find helpful in engaging in difficult situations related to race. I created the acronym PAIRS™ to help me remember each skill. The letters stand for pan, ask, interrupt, relate, and share. I first panned or scanned the room and noticed an increase in tension after his comment. I asked about his intent as a way to interrupt the dynamic and not stay silent as I heard a phrase that I knew was a racist trigger regardless of his conscious intent. I started by letting him know I was inviting him to say more about his intention and then related in by acknowledging how I had said that phrase before as well. I then asked if he knew this was a trigger phrase and invited him to scan the audience to check to see if he could pan racial identities and differences among people. I followed up by asking him to share more about his intent and related in by joining him in his vision. At that point, I shared my thoughts about the probable negative impact of his using that term in the current national context as well as my thoughts on how white allies need to show up. I then invited others to share their feelings and reactions. There are many additional ways to use these PAIRS™ tools. I have included a more detailed description and examples of these skills on my website, www.drkathyobear.com/racebook.

I will never know for sure, but I believe this participant would have shut down and missed this opportunity to learn if I had more directly confronted his comments by saying, "That's a trigger phrase" or "That's a racist term." In the past when I have interrupted a racist dynamic more aggressively, I most often lost the chance for meaningful dialogue or change. I believe my past approaches were short-sighted and potentially harmful to others. I may have gotten an ego-hit from showing up as the "good white," but I probably would never have another chance to engage this person again to deepen our relationship or further learning and growth. And most disturbing to me, I modeled behaviors that may have given other whites permission to be overly aggressive as they confront other whites in similarly unproductive ways. I am deeply committed to "leave no one behind," and I intentionally try to build a connection with other white people who have just said something offensive to create a container within which they can deepen awareness and stay involved in the learning process.

Don't get me wrong; there are still times I feel so triggered by comments and behaviors from whites that I want to "take them out" like I used to! In those moments, it helps me to remember all the people of color and other whites who gave me such love and grace when I made racist comments and helped me move through the depths of my embarrassment, guilt, and shame to recognize the impact of my behavior and learn new ways to engage. I am paying down a debt I can never repay, and I owe it to other white people to show up in love and compassion as I hold them accountable to change their behaviors. In chapter 7, I share a wide variety of additional ways to respond in different "What if?" scenarios.

But before we can consistently engage others effectively, we need to have the humility to realize we need to change our racist attitudes and behaviors and then find the willingness, courage, and commitment to speak up.

CHAPTER 4
WHY WOULD WHITES
WANT TO CHANGE?

"If you have come here to help me, you are wasting your time.
But if you have come because your liberation is bound up
with mine, then let us work together."
- Lilla Watson

I didn't understand this quote for a long time. I had to do a significant depth of healing work before I could shift from my racist stance of helping people of color to one of partnering. A key step in my process was recognizing the debilitating costs of racism for whites. Let me be clear. I am not saying that whites experience racism or that the costs are at all similar to the vast devastating and deadly effects of racism for people of color. Yet, there is a powerful negative impact of racism on whites, and until we realize this and see our liberation completely connected with that of people of color, we will continue to drop in and drop out of change efforts to suit our own needs and convenience.

In this chapter, I identify what I believe can help whites become willing to change. The first step is to recognize and admit we have racial bias. Next, it is critical we examine the costs of believing and acting on these racial prejudices. A final crucial step is to identify reasons that motivate us to dismantle racism that are powerful enough to sustain us for the long haul as well as the benefits of working for racial justice.

Harvard Implicit Bias Test

I had a moment of humility that I hadn't expected. A colleague told me about the Harvard Implicit Bias Test, and I thought it would be a good resource to recommend to participants in my workshops. I didn't know much about it, so I went to the website to take the test https://implicit.harvard.edu/implicit/takeatest.html.

Looking back, I now realize I mistakenly thought I would score as very bias-free given all my self-work on whiteness and the racial justice work I have done over the years. You can imagine my shock and disbelief when the results showed I had negative prejudice towards African Americans. I was somewhat indignant and quickly started to critique the methodology of the test because it couldn't be accurate! The truth is, all I needed to do was to get really honest with myself and recount the recent moments where I had thought racist stereotypes, like when I was waiting for my luggage at an airport and I assumed the black men walking by were Sky Caps, but when I looked a second time, I realized they were passengers on the flight with me. I could continue to list numerous other examples, but here is the bottom line: If I am honest with myself, I become very aware of how often I think racist thoughts, and yet I still was so indignant as I challenged the validity of the Harvard

Implicit Bias Test. I wonder how many white people are like me, always looking for ways to deny the reality of our racist beliefs?

I highly encourage you to take a break from reading right now and go to this website to take the Implicit Bias Test: https://implicit.harvard.edu/implicit/takeatest.html. In addition to the one I took, "Race," the site lists a number of additional tests related to race and racism, including: Asian American, Native American, Arab-Muslim, and Skin-tone. After you get your results, I hope you journal your thoughts, feelings, and reactions so, like me, you will have a good story to tell other whites as you support and coach them in their learning and development.

I felt so humble after reviewing the results. In that place of humility, I was far more open to doing the depth of self-work to identify the racist beliefs I have and the racist behaviors I still participate in, even though it can be a painful process. The gift of the harshness of looking in the mirror provides the fuel to continually do the necessary work to first admit these biases and then to continually put ourselves in uncomfortable situations where we unlearn the racist messages we were taught and relearn the truth about race, racism, white privilege, and white supremacy.

If you are like me, then you need to come from a place of humility to find the willingness to stay in this process. I need daily reminders to constantly check my arrogance and sense of entitlement so I can approach this healing process as a new beginner. I had to recognize and admit that

I was relatively incompetent as a white change agent and that, in fact, I was often doing harm through my actions and attitudes. I had to acknowledge how little I really knew or understood about racism and white supremacy before I could be truly open to this transformational process of learning and unlearning. I only got to this level of willingness from having that deeply triggering, humiliating experience at the Development Lab. I hope you find your way to this new beginning in a far less painful way.

Costs of Racism for Whites

Why would any white person work for racial justice? Why would we constantly put ourselves in the position to have to look at white privilege, recognize our racist attitudes and behaviors, and often get criticized by people of color for not doing enough as well as by many whites for being a race traitor? Why would we choose to feel such depths of guilt and shame? I have been asked these questions many times and often thought them myself over the years. It took me quite a while, but I now see the many costs of racism that I experience from this system of white supremacy and white privilege. All of the undeserved access, power, resources, and opportunities I have received as a white person have come with a heavy price. When I truly acknowledge these costs, I find more energy and commitment to stay in the work for racial justice.

One of the more painful costs is how white people live in such isolation from people of color and other whites. We tend to keep our distance by always walking on eggshells, avoiding situations where we might feel anxious or incompetent, and staying silent for fear of being called racist. As a result, we do not show up as our authentic selves and often have very superficial relationships with people of color in our organizations and in our personal lives. I know I have wasted so much time and energy fronting and performing around people of color, feeling awkward and uncomfortable in the process. People of color clearly notice these dynamics and then have even more reason to distrust us and doubt the sincerity of what we say. We often live in very separate worlds at work, at home, and in the community.

Many white people tell me they have few, if any, white friends and colleagues to talk with about issues of race and racism. They feel so alone in their work and personal lives. They have a long list of former friends and colleagues whom they have left behind because they could no longer bear engaging with them given their friends' racist attitudes and behaviors. We can try to blame others, but I believe we need to look at our part in this dynamic and acknowledge all the times we have judged other whites as clueless and backed away so we wouldn't be associated with anyone who might do something racist. As a result, we get to cling to the illusion that we are a "good white person."

Our relationships with our family and spouses are damaged as well. Most everyone in the white caucuses I facilitate have painful stories of fighting with white members of their family at holiday celebrations and feeling so angry and alienated from people they have loved and looked up to much of their lives. The psychic pain of damaging these connections and losing this level of respect for loved ones is almost unimaginable. In addition, many whites express deep despair as they acknowledge the racist attitudes and actions of their intimate partners and realize they can no longer be involved with someone who is so actively racist. Many feel lost and rudderless as they imagine their future without the family, friends, and partners they now have in their lives.

There are many additional costs of racism for whites who work and collude in racist organizations. Teams are often under-functioning. Given all the microaggressions from white colleagues, people of color may be hesitant to share their ideas, creative thoughts, and concerns, knowing the probability that they will be criticized, overlooked, or punished for their contributions. Some white people may hold back from engaging in authentic conversations or difficult dialogues for fear of being seen as racist and damaging their reputation or future in the organization. When people work in a culture of fear and are waiting for the next shoe to drop, we all lose from lower productivity, lack of innovation, unproductive conflict, mediocre customer service, and stunted professional development.

While many organizations state they want to attract and retain more people of color, the reality is that most have created a revolving door where they hire people of color, yet many of these employees leave within 1-3 years due to the toxic, racist environment. White leaders might be more concerned about the racist dynamics in their organizations if they ever saw the actual financial loss incurred from hiring, training, and developing talent who consistently turn over, as well as costs from the serious disruption in productivity and burnout when employees leave and those left behind have to pick up time-consuming additional responsibilities. Leaders might have even more concern and willingness to shift racist dynamics if they could calculate the cost of lost revenue from their failure to retain more customers of color and successfully access emerging markets.

White people carry, often unconsciously, a significant amount of stress from trying to succeed in organizations that require adherence to white cultural norms and ways of being. We often live in restricted, constrained ways that are not in our own best interest. It is easy to feel burned out and become less effective over time from having to always compete with other colleagues, hold in your emotions to appear logical and rational, produce vast quantities of work, live with the constant sense of urgency and perfectionism, and always worry that you are not good enough (Okun, 2001).

There are also significant costs from having learned a one-dimensional view of history. We lost our true history while we were taught racist information about how whites were the superior race who civilized the world, freed the slaves, and built a country to ensure liberty and justice, peace and prosperity for all. When we begin to learn the truth about how white people intentionally committed genocide and slaughtered people of color while creating racist systems to guarantee whites access to power and privilege, we often lose pride in our country and feel deeply ashamed of being white. We feel lost and powerless and overwhelmed with guilt.

One reason it is hard to see any way forward is we were denied access to the truth about the role of white people over the centuries who worked in partnership with people of color to create social change and challenge racism. Those who search and find this lost history can gain deep inspiration, motivation, and insight from these role models about how to live a life of integrity as a white change agent today.

Few white people ever learn the full impact of the ravages of racism in school or from the media. We remain content, comfortable, and complacent in our ignorance and cannot begin to understand why people of color feel so angry or demand faster, more meaningful change. We have been numbed out by the Novocain of white privilege. If and when it begins to wear off, we get glimpses of the devastation and seemingly irreparable harm whites have caused through racism as well as the unearned privileges we receive at the expense and exploitation of people of color.

At this point, most whites have two choices for how to deal with this debilitating pain. We can choose to sit in this deep anguish, feel our feelings, and use them to fuel new efforts to learn more, unlearn racist training, and discover how to do our part to dismantle racism. Unfortunately, too few whites choose this path. Most, in my opinion, choose instead to find more ways to numb out and distract ourselves so we can pretend not to see the reality right in front of us.

This second option is a path of self-destruction because once we begin to see the truth, we cannot ever truly forget. We will always carry the heavy burden of white guilt and shame and need ever more powerful ways to try to forget, including blaming people of color for the racism they experience. No matter how we try, we still carry the heavy burden of all these emotions and fears into everything we do.

Another deeply impactful cost of racism for white people is the corroding impact of believing racist stereotypes and prejudice. It is severely debilitating for whites to carry this level of fear, distrust, and hatred towards people of color. These racist attitudes result in so much negativity in our lives and poison our relationships with others and with ourselves. We are weighed down by the illusion of danger and constantly fear for our safety. We limit our choices of where we live and work, who our friends are, where our children go to school, where we worship, what media and news we listen to, and what activities we do. We live in constant fear that people of color will do to us what we have done to them over the centuries. As a result, we create such segregated lives that we wall ourselves off from over 85% of the world's population. In my experience, few white people ever realize how severely limited and narrow our lives truly are.

A resulting cost is we trust those we should really fear. Research consistently shows that we are more likely to experience violence and crime from people of our own racial background. Yet despite clear data, whites continue to fear people of color and trust whites. I lived in an urban area for about four years where I was one of a very few white people in a radius of a dozen blocks from our apartment. While initially wary and acting out of racist stereotypes, after a few months I realized that I was perfectly safe in that neighborhood. The irony is that the only time I felt in danger was one afternoon when I was walking in a predominantly white, upper middle class area about a mile from where we lived. I was going to an appointment and was lost in thought when I had a sense I needed to pay attention. As I turned to look behind me, I noticed a white man walking way too close to me. I quickly scanned the area and saw no one else nearby and so jogged ahead to the end of the block and crossed the street. Within a moment I realized he was again walking very close behind me, so I sprinted ahead until I got nearer to other people. I experienced his behavior as far more threatening than anything I encountered in the neighborhood where I lived. We have been taught we can trust those who look like us, when in reality that is where the most danger can lie.

Growing up in this racist culture has left whites with the illusion of superiority and an over-inflated sense of self. Consciously or unconsciously, we tend to believe we are smarter, better, and more deserving than people of color. So much of our sense of self and self-esteem is based on this racist fabrication, and we are crushed when we realize this is all a lie. I clearly remember beginning to wake up to this truth and felt devastated as I began to question everything in my life: Was I as smart as I was led to believe? Did I get those promotions based on my competence or due to white privilege? Do I have any authentic relationships with people of color? If I truly had to compete with people of color, would I ever get another job? I can't find the words to explain how debilitating it was to truly question if I ever was as good and competent as I once thought.

When I first sat in the painful reality of racism and white privilege, I lost my self-confidence and the pendulum of my self-esteem swung all the way to the other end where I felt completely incompetent and worthless as a change agent. I believe this state is as unproductive as wallowing in our white guilt and shame. We stay stuck, choosing to believe we are powerlessness, as we do little to nothing to create racial justice. And it is also a lie. With time, I was able to recognize some of the useful knowledge and skills I did have, and as I chose courage, I kept learning and developing a larger toolkit as a change agent. This took some time, and I still am working to fill the deep gap in my knowledge, skill, and competence that I never learned as a white person.

Another cost of racism to most whites is we do not have the life experiences and education to develop the critical capacity to succeed and serve in an increasingly diverse, global marketplace. The irony is, for all of the illusion of superiority, we are not very competent or prepared to work effectively on diverse teams, much less lead multicultural organizations. We may find ourselves in leadership positions, but if we are honest with ourselves, we feel like a fraud and may live in fear that we will be found out as incompetent. We rarely have the skills to create inclusive environments, confront and shift racist comments and actions, or eliminate institutional racism from policies, practices and services. Since racism results in over-valuing whites and significantly limiting the number of people of color in leadership, many white people are promoted past their competence and are sometimes ineffective, if not dangerous, leaders. White employees often describe the ineptitude of their white supervisors, managers and executives. The negative impact on organizational and human resources is significant.

Racism has long survived from a "divide and conquer" approach perpetuated by the elite. As long as whites and people of color are kept separate, we can never join forces to dismantle the oppressive organizations that negatively impact us all. The lack of capacity of whites to build solidarity across race prevents us from organizing and working together to create truly inclusive institutions or to challenge exploitive, oppressive actions and policies that hurt us all. In my experience, if leaders create racist policies and practices as well as allow racist behaviors to go unaddressed, they are also likely to perpetuate organizational dynamics that are sexist, classist, heterosexist, and ableist, as well as many other forms of oppression.

One of the most painful costs of racism for me was my lost humanity. I sold my soul for white privilege, the illusion of superiority, and all the comfort and ease these brought me in my life. I had to wall off my heart in order to live with the dissonance of seeing the devastations of racism in the lives of people of color while recognizing the unearned white privilege I received. I had to believe and nurture racist beliefs in order to rationalize why I and so many white people were doing so well while the majority of people of color in this country and around the world live in poverty or with far fewer resources and opportunities than most whites. I had to find ways to justify why I so often stayed silent and did not confront racist dynamics, protecting my position and privilege while I threw people of color under the bus. I traded my humanity for comfort, prosperity, white privilege, and status. I believed all the lies and excuses for my success and came to accept that I rightfully deserved all the benefits I received from racism.

What's In It For Me?

In order to maintain the level of energy and persistence we need to be effective white allies, we have to find a deep sense of passion and motivation to be resilient in this work. Unfortunately, I looked in the wrong place in the beginning.

A common trap I fell into as a white ally was wanting to help people of color. For years, I never questioned my motivation or recognized how it was rooted in the racist belief that people of color were deficient and incapable of creating change on their own and, therefore, needed my help. There are several more reasons this approach was both unproductive and unsustainable. I now realize that I was motivated to help to lessen my feelings of guilt and shame. As long as I thought I was doing some good, I could distract myself with frenetic activity and not have to sit with all these painful feelings or acknowledge the negative impact of my racist behaviors. The problem was, when I didn't feel this depth of guilt or shame, I lost my motivation to stay committed and did very little to work for racial justice.

Another problem with this patronizing approach of helping people of color is that I came from a deficit model and only focused on how racism devastated the lives of people of color. I was fixated on correcting these problems and fixing what I thought were the deficits of people of color. I never looked at how whiteness and internalized dominance were showing up in my actions and how I was part of the problem. I tried to present myself as the white savior, all the while expecting and demanding that people of color constantly recognize and thank me for all that I was doing for them. When I didn't feel they were giving me enough accolades and praise, I resented people of color for not acknowledging and appreciating me enough. I used this as an excuse to stop focusing as much on the dynamics of race and racism. I actually feel a little sick as I write this section and admit the truth of my experience.

I had so little endurance and persistence when I came from this deficit stance of helping. As soon as someone of color expressed any frustration towards me or criticized my efforts, I again thought, "I'm damned if I do, and damned if I don't! If I can't do this right enough for them, then why bother?" All too often I chose to sit in this place of self-pity and resentment thinking, "I work so hard and no one appreciates me!" As a result, my motivation to be a white ally fizzled quickly and I distracted myself with other matters.

Coming from the illusion that we are helping people of color is never sustainable. Whites need to find deeper, more personal reasons to stay committed to the work of racial justice or we will continually use our white privilege to drop out when anything gets too hard. I believe we need to become grounded in how racism and white supremacy hurt us and find our self-interest to stay in the work for the long haul.

Benefits of Working for Racial Justice

Why would white people work for racial justice? We work for racial justice because our survival depends on our collective ability to shatter racism and reclaim our humanity. When whites choose courage and refuse to collude and perpetuate racist dynamics, they deepen their capacity to develop authentic, meaningful relationships with people of color and other whites. Through these coalitions we can create more inclusive organizations that support the success of all members and create innovative products and services that truly benefit everyone's welfare. We can regain a sense of pride in our work and in ourselves. We can finally live with integrity, look ourselves in the mirror, and know we are doing all we can to dismantle racism and create liberation for all. Whites gain inner strength and a sense of purpose from being an active part of creating change, from working in multiracial organizations committed to racial justice, and from knowing we are finally a part of the solution.

Through these efforts we begin to develop a new friendship circle and a true community of loving colleagues. And if you are like me, your most intimate relationships will be forever changed as you show up authentically engaging issues of race and racism every day and together becoming a powerful team and source of support for each other's work in the world.

White people will feel such relief from guilt and shame as we make our own personal reparations and amends for the racist comments and actions in our past. As we pay it forward in our work with other whites, we feel energized as we honestly share our stories of racist actions to support other whites on their journey to healing and self-awareness.

As we intentionally broaden our network of white allies and colleagues and build a community of support for our own development, we find so many more people with whom we can be honest and vulnerable and from whom we can get the coaching and role modeling we need to stay active on this journey of liberation.

One of the greatest gifts of doing my own self-work and staying committed to racial justice has been the opportunity to develop authentic relationships with people of color, colleagues and friends with whom I can show up more fully and be myself. Those times when my comments have crossed a line and had a negative impact, I have, mostly, been able to stay present and engage effectively to understand the impact of my racist comment or action, own my part, and then make amends through changing my behavior. Instead of my fear coming true that I would ruin these friendships, I have found that these honest conversations have actually strengthened my relationships with people of color and deepened the trust between us.

Maybe most fulfilling is that we can now be the role model, coach, and leader for other white people that we so desperately needed when we were younger. If we truly invest in our own self-work, we may be able to make a significant difference in the lives of others and support them on their journey to wholeness as they unlearn racist beliefs and learn the tools, skills and attitudes to become effective change agents in their own right. As we do our part to dismantle internalized dominance and racist practices in ourselves, in others, and in our organizations, we can take our place in a long line of whites over the centuries who have committed themselves to racial justice and learned to partner with people of color to create liberation and justice for all. And in the process, we can reclaim our humanity.

The challenge is, if you are like me, once I realized I desperately needed and wanted to change, I didn't know where to begin or how to move forward.

CHAPTER 5
HOW DO I GET
THERE FROM HERE

After I was confronted on my racist behaviors at the Development Lab, I felt lost and unmoored. I had no idea what to do or how to move forward. I felt devastated and terrified that I had ruined my career as a consultant and trainer. Fortunately, a white mentor spent some time with me to debrief the experience and helped me begin to make meaning of the feedback I received and what I needed to do next. While colleagues of color offered support as well, I was too ashamed to hear and accept their outreach. This was one of the costs of choosing to stay frozen in white fragility (DiAngelo, 2011). This term refers to the hyper-sensitivity and defensiveness of white people when we experience someone naming our racist behavior. White fragility keeps white people stuck in our negative emotions of guilt, helplessness, and defensiveness. It allows us to avoid accepting the reality of our racist behavior and often results in our blaming people of color instead of looking at the truth of our actions.

Without the support of a white mentor at that critical time in my life, I am not sure if I would have made any progress or continued on my journey as a white change agent. I may have chosen to stay stuck in feelings of deep guilt, shame, embarrassment, and self-pity. I might have continued to do basic diversity training, but I doubt I would have been on the path I am on today. This white mentor shared her own struggles in looking at her racism and provided hope that although I felt like a horrible human being, I wasn't. She challenged me to accept the feedback and do more self-work, to learn about white privilege, racist attitudes, and internalized dominance. She helped me understand this was the necessary journey if I really wanted to become the person I hoped to be. I may never know why she cared enough to keep coaching me over those next years or why she invested so much of herself to help me recover, heal, and grow. But I am eternally grateful and hope I honor her through my actions with other whites today.

Path to Competence™

I believe it is critical that whites take a personal inventory and deeply reflect on their racial journey over their lives. It is important to identify the ways we were socialized in this racist culture and the choices we made to perpetuate the status quo as well as the times we chose courage to heal from internalized dominance and challenge racist dynamics in ourselves, in others, and in our organizations.

The model Path to Competence™, developed by Drs. Delyte Frost and Jack Gant, has been a powerful tool to help me make meaning of my life experiences as a raced being. Adapted from Abraham Maslow's Conscious-Unconscious Competence model, the Path to Competence™ gave me a road map to identify where I have come from and a plan for how to move forward. There are five key elements in this transformational process: Box of Denial, Box of Judgement, Box of Fear, Box of Engagement, and Box of Competence (Gant, 2013; Riley & Frost, 2009).

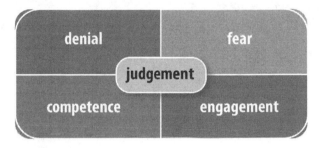

Path to Competence™
Moving to Competence with Us/Them

Below, I illustrate examples of how this model applies to my own experience.

Box of Denial

During that Development Lab, though I never could have admitted it at the time, my racist actions reflected how I was in the Box of Denial. I was both unaware and very ineffective as a white change agent. I knew I was white and had a good bit of conceptual knowledge about race and racism, but I couldn't recognize the common patterns of racist dynamics and microaggressions that occur as a result of the systems of racism in organizations and society or from my own individual actions. I was completely unaware of how my behaviors were rooted in racist beliefs and stereotypes. I couldn't recognize the blatant ways I acted out of my privileged status or how my racist behaviors negatively impacted colleagues of color. I still thought of myself only as an individual, a well-intended white person. I had a bunch of perfectly logical explanations for why my actions had nothing to do with race, when in reality, I had responded in very typical privileged, racist ways.

Box of Judgement

As a result of the feedback I received during and after the Development Lab, I soon found myself in another element of the Path to Competence™, the Box of Judgement, where I was stuck in blame and shame. I first blamed my colleagues of color for misunderstanding situations and over-reacting, though I soon became mired in the quicksand of deep embarrassment and shame and was swirling in white fragility (DiAngelo, 2011). I berated myself for my actions, and for several years I couldn't talk about the incidents except with my mentor and my intimate partner. I stuffed my emotions, hid my shame, and completely avoided any memory or mention of that entire experience. As you can imagine, that was a heavy burden to carry and conceal.

Though I was completely unaware of these dynamics at the time, I now see that one of the only ways I got any relief from my deep shame was to blame and shame other white people as I aggressively confronted them on their racist behaviors. As long as I could focus on others and judge them, I could avoid focusing on myself. I thought I was doing good work, when in reality, I was rarely very helpful. In fact, my actions may have interfered with the growth and development of the white people with whom I interacted. I was coming out of negative and selfish intentions: trying to prove I was a good white person at their expense. I aggressively called them out with a judgmental, self-righteous energy to try to convince myself that I was better than they were, trying to bury the truth about my past and current racist behaviors. I am most deeply pained knowing that many of those white people may have then replicated my incompetent behaviors with other whites.

Box of Fear

Around that time, I was also operating out of another element on the Path to Competence™, the Box of Fear. My comments and reactions were most often very ineffective, even though I was more aware of dynamics of race and racism. I was speaking up more in meetings, white caucuses, and my other training sessions, but my interventions were not very useful. I had not developed any more capacity or skill as a white ally. I was always walking on eggshells in my interactions with people of color and in mixed race groups. I lived in fear that I would say something racist and be called out on my racist behaviors. While I saw more racist dynamics occur around me, I was very hesitant to respond for fear of doing it wrong, saying something offensive, or making things worse. I often stayed silent and colluded in order to maintain the illusion that I was a good white ally.

I may not have progressed along the Path to Competence™ much further except for the bravery of a white intern at SJTI. I am deeply grateful that she confronted me on my ineffective, more hostile facilitation style in a white caucus session. Don't get me wrong. I was enraged at the time and resisted her feedback. But she held up a mirror to me and over time, I got honest with myself about the harm I was doing in caucuses, as well as in mixed race conversations. Around that same time, I was stopped in my tracks when I saw a billboard advertising Listerine mouthwash that read, "Less intense, just as effective." This message went right through me like a bolt of lightning. Over time and with some healing work, I began to significantly shift how I facilitated white caucuses. I became far less intense and aggressive and instead focused on building a community of support and accountability with other whites. I was only able to begin this transition after I started to do a deeper layer of healing work on myself, what I call self-work.

I took a more honest look at my life and acknowledged the racist attitudes and stereotypes I still held onto. I admitted the negative impact of my past racist behaviors and no longer tried to stuff the deep grief and embarrassment I felt. Somewhere along this path to accepting the truth about myself, I began to feel some forgiveness for all I had done before and found a renewed sense of commitment to change my behaviors in the future.

One of the biggest surprises in this process was the feeling of compassion I began to experience for myself and for other white people for the destructive impact of the racist socialization in our lives. I felt deep grief for how I had traded my humanity for the illusion of superiority and white privilege, and I discovered a new ground of being from which to engage other whites. I believe the first step to healing internalized dominance is to admit and own the truth about our racist behaviors and then to sit with the pain of realizing the impact we have had on people of color. This process is about acceptance, not judgment or shame.

The more I did my self-work, the more willing I became to talk about my racist behaviors and attitudes in white caucuses, meetings, and other trainings. I began to share from a place of growing humility, not out of humiliation or shame. The more I shared, the more energy I had to keep digging into my past and current life to root out even more racist attitudes that fueled my behaviors. I had somehow stumbled onto a path to healing.

I soon realized that the more I talked about my racist attitudes and actions, the more the other white participants seemed willing to look at themselves and talk about their own experiences. The more they shared, the more I felt connected to them at a deeper emotional level. As people told their stories, I saw myself in each one of them. In the past when I confronted and judged other white people, I had felt so alone and isolated. As I began to engage out of more humility, compassion, and deepening honesty, I finally found community.

Box of Engagement

Over the years, I began to operate more out of the Box of Engagement than either the Box of Fear or Judgment, though I can quickly be back to choosing fear or judgement in a split second! In the Box of Engagement, I was developing more skills and capacity to effectively engage other whites as well as to respond more productively in multiracial groups. I still had to consciously think about what I was doing and work to keep an intentional focus on dynamics of race and racism, but over time, I continued to broaden my skill set and confidence as a white ally.

Somewhere along the way I became better at listening and considering the feedback of others. Occasionally, I asked other white people and people of color for reflections about the impact of my actions on them and others. I still initially bristle when others give me unsolicited feedback, but I have truly benefitted when I have chosen to pause, take a deep breath, trust the process, and view their feedback as a gift and an important lesson I need to learn.

I believe one of the most critical aspects of this journey is to stay in continuous dialogue and connection with other white allies. Every time I talk face-to-face or participate in a virtual gathering with other whites, I get to see myself in their stories, deepen my self-awareness as I get honest with them, and hold myself more accountable for my thoughts, attitudes, and actions.

Box of Competence

When people are operating out of the final element in the Path to Competence™, the Box of Competence, they are responding out of unconscious competence. I have moments in this space when I am in the flow and respond effectively without much planning or thought. When white people are in this place, they consistently respond in useful ways, and if they make a mistake, they readily own their impact and make amends. They are committed to lifelong learning about race, racism, white privilege, and internalized dominance and continually do their own self-work in order to show up as a clear, effective instrument of change.

The Path to Competence™ has been a powerful map to guide my journey. I am deeply grateful to Delyte Frost and Jack Gant for their wisdom and their willingness to share this model with others. It has been especially useful when I find myself regressing at times. As soon as I recognize I am in the Box of Judgement and shaming myself or others or I am in the Box of Fear and walking on eggshells and reacting less effectively, I know what I need to do to be more effective in that moment. Usually, it means I need to get honest and authentically share what I am feeling and thinking.

Suggested Competencies for White Change Agents

There is a wide range of competencies that I believe whites can deepen on their own or in community with other whites as they develop along the Path to Competence™. For a fuller list, you can download the worksheet, "Suggested Competencies for White Allies," on my website, www. drkathyobear.com/racebook. While this is not a comprehensive list, my hope is that it is a useful tool to assess your current level of competence and identify goals for your professional development. It may also be a good resource in learning communities for white people to plan their discussion topics and skill practice sessions. I want to highlight some competencies that have helped me in my work as a white change agent.

Study the dynamics and manifestations of race and racism

White people need to have a deep understanding of the history of race and racism in the U.S. and around the world so we can begin to see how white culture and white supremacy were created to privilege white people at the expense of basic human rights for people of color. While it can be incredibly painful to read books or watch movies about slavery, genocide, apartheid, internment camps, lynchings, environmental racism, and the myriad of other ways white people have oppressed and still do intentionally oppress people of color to maintain whiteness and white privilege, we need to stay vigilant and aware of the violence of racism in order to open our hearts, keep our minds fresh, and find a deep source of passion and commitment to stay in the work.

Additionally, it is critical that whites continuously deepen their understanding of the current examples of racism in society, including the legal system, the school to prison pipeline, immigration policies and practices, and the militarization of police forces. It is also essential for white people to study how racism and white supremacy are embedded into every U.S. institution, including education, housing, employment, heath care, religious institutions, and the media.

Recognize white privilege

Another key competency is to recognize the vast examples of white privilege that we receive each and every day and how our current success as white people is directly connected to white privilege. It is critical we develop the capacity and courage to speak up when we notice examples of white privilege in our organizations and in our own lives. I describe this concept in greater depth in Chapter 6.

Recognize and shift white culture in organizations

It is also important that we recognize how white culture is infused into organizational practices and standards about what is professional and effective as well as how it is enforced through a system of rewards and punishments. In addition, it is critical that we develop the capacity to interrupt these white cultural norms when they negatively impact others and undermine organizational effectiveness.

We need to develop inclusive, productive ways to engage each other and work together that honor the values and needs of all members. (I talk more about white culture in Chapter 6)

Recognize and interrupt microaggressions

The capacity to recognize racist comments and actions is a critical competency for white allies. We need to increase our skills and willingness to effectively interrupt our own racist behaviors as well as those of others. In this process, it is important that whites recognize and accept the probable costs we will experience if we choose to use our white privilege to speak up and challenge racist dynamics.

Engage resistance

A more challenging set of tools may be the ability to effectively engage resistance from whites who passively or actively support the racist status quo in organizations and in society. They may still believe white culture and racist practices are good for business and should be the norm in organizations. A key skill set is the capacity to recognize and engage whites who use coded language to try to maintain the racist status quo and their privileged positions in organizations. This requires the ability to consistently keep race on our screen in all of our interactions as we analyze programs, policies, practices, and services to ensure they meet the needs of both people of color and white people. To do this, we need the capacity and courage to keep race on the table as one possible factor that could be influencing every dynamic and interaction we experience.

Build connections with other white people

We then need the ability and willingness to stay engaged in dialogue with other whites. Instead of distancing ourselves, we need to build meaningful relationships with white colleagues to support our collective awareness and skill development as allies. There are a number of interpersonal tools I use in white caucuses that we can use in everyday interactions to build meaningful relationships with other whites. I discuss these in more detail later in this chapter.

Deepening our capacity to relate in and to see ourselves in the stories and actions of other white people is a critical capacity for having productive conversations. Additionally, the ability to use self-disclosure to build trust and deepen learning and self-awareness is also essential for effective engagement. Whites can also develop their capacity to use the Ladder of Fear™ to dig underneath feelings and resistance to identify core fears and issues driving unproductive behaviors. I describe the Ladder of Fear™ in greater detail later in this chapter. Finally, it is important to develop the capacity and resilience to stay present to ourselves as we express our emotions in triggering situations.

Recognize the impact of racist actions

A difficult set of skills for me to develop was the capacity to help white people explore the (un)intended impact of their racist comments and behaviors. These tools include the ability to facilitate meaningful dialogue when whites commonly resist by only focusing on their intent.

Engage out of compassion

Finally, it is essential that we consistently do enough of our own self-work and healing to engage other whites out of a space of compassion and care while we also hold them accountable for efforts to change their racist values, attitudes, and behaviors. As we identify the multitude of times we have acted out of internalized dominance and racist attitudes, we may develop the necessary humility to connect with whites as peers and colleagues as we support each other's healing and growth.

We must be vigilant and persistent as white change agents as we continually deepen our capacity to create greater racial justice. Unlearning racism is a lifelong process of healing and re-education. I hope you choose to stay in it for the long haul. If you do, I guarantee that when you wake up each day and look in the mirror, you will realize you are closer to living a life of integrity and purpose.

Participate in White Affinity Groups

While I deeply believe it is critical to our development that whites actively participate in white affinity spaces, I don't want you to have the misconception that I readily embraced white caucus work from the start. I remember feeling deep resistance and anxiety the first time I sat in a group of all white people during a weekend workshop on racism. I thought it would be such a waste of time: How could I learn anything without people of color in the room? Whites are so boring! And I probably did waste that experience as I judged other white people and kept myself distant from them and from myself. I stayed quiet and under the radar in hopes that no one would call me out as racist.

Ways to Create a Learning Environment in White Caucuses

I facilitated my first white caucus in 1998 when we changed our focus at SJTI and held our first race immersion experience. Over the years I have learned ways to create this sacred container to support white people in their healing, growth, and development. As much as I work to create a compassionate space for authentic engagement, many white people seem to enter caucuses feeling a significant degree of discomfort and fear. I have come to expect the predictable reactions of white fragility, including defensiveness, fear, shame, and resistance to talking about whiteness, white privilege, and our own racist attitudes and behaviors (DiAngelo, 2011).

I believe it helps when I frame the caucus by talking about some of my initial reactions in early white caucuses as well as stating my intentions as the facilitator and holder of the process. I notice some white people tend to relax a bit as I talk about my intent to create a brave space where we all can get honest about ways our socialization in this racist culture shows up in our often unconscious treatment of people of color and other whites. I talk about how lonely I have felt without a community of white people doing work on our racism and how connected I often feel in these white caucuses as we deepen our capacity to authentically share, relate, and see ourselves in each other's stories and experiences. I clearly state how I intend to leave no one behind as I commit to not judging others or distancing myself from them as I have in the past when I was trying to show up as the good white person to gain the approval of people of color. In summary, I ask people to be real, relate to what others share, lean into discomfort, and choose courage to say the unsaid, what they are deeply afraid to admit to us or to themselves.

Each time I name one of these intentions or common dynamics of white people, I ask if people can relate to me, and many often do. This process of "relating in" sets the tone for new ways of engaging as white people that are counter to white cultural norms. Instead of competing to be seen as the most evolved white person or attacking each other to prove we are not racist, I offer a way to connect and relate to each other as we build a community of supportive white colleagues. Together, we create a learning environment of compassion and care as we also hold each other accountable to recognize and shift our racist attitudes and behaviors. I am amazed with each white caucus as I witness the depth of self-work and healing that manifests in this type of loving space of accountability. We all learn from each other as we create this moment of true community.

Facilitating White Caucuses
There are a number of techniques I commonly use in white caucuses. As we begin, I facilitate a process for us to share

and relate into each other's feelings in the moment. I invite all the participants to write whatever they are feeling on a slip of paper: One word or feeling phrase and then a sentence to give some context for each of the feelings they can identify. Most people use 5-7 pieces of paper to express the breadth and depth of their emotions. I then ask them to scrunch them up and throw them into the center of the circle as I invite a few folks to mix them all up and redistribute them to everyone. We then read each piece of paper aloud, one at a time, without any comment or response. I invite the participants to see themselves in each item read aloud and relate to what was shared. The impact of this process has always been powerful. Most whites seem to be much more fully in their bodies and more present as they realize how many others share their feelings of fear, remorse, shame, anger, and embarrassment. They realize they are not alone and that people are willing to be honest, at least in this anonymous activity.

I next ask people to identify themes they heard during the read-out and then invite someone to start by sharing how they related to what they heard. This is where any predictability of the process ends. I never know how people will show up. I do my best to facilitate the process to create deepening honesty and connection to self and others as we slowly build a circle of increasing trust and vulnerability.

I consistently nudge people, gently, to get out of their heads and into their bodies and emotions. Deep healing work as white people is not about conceptual knowledge, in my opinion. Staying in our heads actually sabotages the possibility of growth.

Ladder of Fear™

I must seem like a broken record as I continually ask people what they are feeling and then nudge them to dig deeper and find the emotions and fears underneath their initial response. I teach and model a tool I call the Ladder of Fear™. When someone seems stuck, I ask, "What are you afraid could happen?" And after their answer, I ask, "And if that were to occur, what else are you afraid of?" Eventually, most people hit a very deep fear and the group can physically feel the shift of energy when they do.

A common deep fear is connected to our concern about losing relationships with friends and family or with colleagues of color and other whites in our lives. If this were to happen, we fear we will be all alone in the world. Another deep fear, that I also relate to, is realizing how incompetent we actually are and how we possibly got jobs and promotions more out of white privilege than our own capabilities. These are very painful, incredibly vulnerable places to sit for most white people. As I work to relate in to everyone who shares and encourage other whites to join in as well, I hope people never feel alone and soon realize how alike we all really are. The details and context of the stories may differ, but our fears, feelings, and racist attitudes and behaviors are all too similar.

Admit Our Racist Attitudes and Actions

The magic of these caucuses is the relief that most white people feel as they honestly share their racist attitudes and behaviors with a group that holds them in love and compassion while we challenge one another to find new ways of thinking and responding. I feel such joy as I watch so many whites shift from staying stuck in guilt, shame, and blame to accepting responsibility for their actions and making a commitment to real change.

As we engage each other in ways that are counter to white cultural practices, we learn alternative ways to show up in our lives. For example, a very common way white people tend to respond to those who just shared a racist behavior is to assume a "holier than thou" stance and tell them how they should have reacted differently. I don't know about you, but I have never reacted well when someone tried to give me advice with what I experience as condescending, self-righteous energy. Any time I sense people are trying to tell others what to do, I interrupt and ask them if they can relate. I nudge them to first share how they relate to the other person and then tell a story of how they have done something similar. I'll then open the conversation to explore what they learned from that experience that has helped them show up differently as a white ally. In this way, they are offering their experience as a gift for anyone to pick up, not telling others how they should act, think and feel.

At the beginning of every white caucus, most participants say they feel lost and stuck, and have no idea how to move forward. About halfway through the four hours of caucuses at SJTI, most begin to see that the only way out is through. We get such relief and healing from admitting the many ways we have thought and acted on racist beliefs. And as we sit together in deep pain as we acknowledge the harm we have caused and continue to create with our racist actions, we begin to see there are other ways we can be far more effective as white people as we partner with people of color to create greater racial justice.

As we continue to build our community, most whites readily share and relate in to each other. You can feel the visceral shift in the room as we move from competing with each other to building connections with love and compassion. We realize how much we can learn from each other and mostly, how much we need each other in this healing process.

Holding Each Other Accountable

I am most delighted by the ways I get to see the white people at SJTI engage each other differently over our last days together. I watch as they admit racist dynamics in the full group, relate in, and leave no one behind as their white peers take a risk and possibly mess up again. They challenge each other more effectively as some of us continue to say and do racist things and then follow-up afterwards to stay in the conversation.

We practice confronting the racist attitudes and actions we see in each other without attacking each other's humanity. We confront because we care too much about each other to let anyone continue to act out of these racist (un)conscious beliefs and negatively impact others and themselves. In the process, we gain new insights, courage, and strategies to respond more effectively to address racist microaggressions and disrupt institutionalized racism in our organizations and in society.

Acknowledge Our Process and Progress

In our last caucus session on the final day at SJTI, I ask participants to reflect on how we built our learning community and then express specific appreciations for what other whites said or did that helped us have authentic dialogue, deepen self-awareness, shift our racist attitudes and behaviors, and increase our capacity as white change agents. As we explore ways participants can integrate their new insights and learning into their work and personal life, I remind them that anything they did or experienced here they can bring back to their organizations and their lives. They just need to find the courage to continue to step up and engage with clarity, humility, and compassion.

At least for this moment in time, many white people experience a true community of white allies, unlike anything they may have ever known. They can now envision what is possible and see new ways to be effective white change agents. After SJTI, I believe many whites intentionally work to create a similar community of white allies in their organizations and in their local region.

My parting hope in our last white caucus is for each person, including myself, to commit to staying in this work for the long haul. We agree to seek out the support and coaching of other whites in times of stress, tension and fear, those times when we want to run away. How do we get there from here? In my experience, the only way out is through, as we work together in authentic community with other white people.

Build a Community of White Allies

At this point, you may want to find a community of white allies to support your continuing growth and development yet have no idea how to do this. There are a number of models I can suggest. Some white people start off by finding or forming a book group to read and discuss articles and books about whiteness, racism, white supremacy, and creating institutional change. Others seek out or create white caucuses that are designed to help participants develop deeper knowledge, self-awareness, and skills to dismantle racism in themselves and their organizations. It may be useful to use social media or the Internet to find or start a group.

One place to start for any group of white allies is to review the work of AWARE LA, https://awarela.wordpress.com. AWARE stands for Alliance of White Anti-Racists Everywhere and there are amazing resources on their website to help start your own chapter.

I truly believe that you can change your life when you have on-going purposeful, meaningful interactions with other white change agents and allies who are actively learning how to partner effectively across race to create greater racial justice. In my experience, you will feel far less powerless and helpless as you deepen your skills and competencies to dismantle racism in a supportive white community. As you build more authentic relationships with other white people, you will have multiple individuals you can call for coaching and support and possibly some nudging and accountability when you stumble or get stuck on your journey.

Choosing the format and learning agenda may differ depending upon the goals and current levels of capacity of group members. It may be useful to use a couple of activities to build a container of trust and honesty, including sharing racist socialization stories and some of the critical incidents in our race journeys.

I always find it helpful to hear specific examples of when other white people have acted out of racist attitudes as I can see myself in their examples and find the courage to share my own. The list of *Common Racist Behaviors and Attitudes of Whites* on my website, www.drkathyobear.com/racebook, may be a useful resource to help people identify and share some of their recent racist actions. The next step might be to talk about times you have spoken up and engaged other white people's racist behaviors, as well as why you chose to collude and stay silent at times. Another powerful way to build capacity is to identify a long list of difficult situations where group members still feel stuck. In subsequent group discussions, it can be powerful for people to first talk about times they mishandled these types of situations and then identify and practice more effective ways to engage and respond for each of these.

As the members of white ally groups deepen their trust and willingness to get honest, it can be useful to set the norm that people can ask for and offer feedback to each other. It may be important to first discuss the common pitfalls of confronting and giving feedback to other white people. All too often I hear stories of how whites have come out of a place of social justice arrogance as they challenged their colleagues. As I noted earlier in this chapter, I can so relate! My hope is that white people can share their own journey to finding a more effective way of engaging each other and also model approaches that are "less intense, just as effective," if not even more effective, in helping other white people look in the mirror.

It may be important for white ally groups to spend some significant time exploring the dynamics of triggering events by first having members share their common triggers and ways they have reacted unproductively in the past. My book *Turn the Tide: Rise Above Toxic, Difficult Situations in the Workplace* may be a useful resource to find new ways of navigating triggered reactions and practice more effective tools to respond in these moments. You can download a free copy of my book on my website, www.drkathyobear. com/book-pdf or order the ebook or paperback on Amazon, www.amazon.com/dp/B01AREQ6K6.

A few additional topics for white ally groups to explore and practice include how to engage other white people when they are triggered or in deep resistance as well as how to effectively respond after you have done something racist. It is also important to frequently discuss and share ways that white allies sustain their energy and commitment to stay on the journey. Once group members have done enough self-work, it can then be useful to identify and strategize how to effectively partner with people of color and other white people to shift institutional racism in organizations.

I hope you give yourself the gift of a loving community of white allies that will hold you accountable for your continued growth and effectiveness as a change agent. Going this alone is a recipe for failure. You will most likely drop out when the going gets tough. Choose, instead, to help create and hold space for other white people to unlearn their racist attitudes and stereotypes, heal from internalized dominance, find the courage to speak up, and develop greater capacity to create racial justice in the world.

CHAPTER 6
CREATING CHANGE AT THE ORGANIZATIONAL LEVEL

I used to believe that all I needed to do as a white ally was to recognize and respond to microaggressions and interrupt racist interpersonal dynamics. Larger concepts such as white privilege and institutional racism were terms I had heard, but I had no real understanding of how these concepts applied to me. While all of the work to interrupt racist dynamics at the individual and interpersonal levels is necessary, it is not sufficient to create meaningful, sustainable change. I have come to believe that there will be no real change until we mobilize sufficient resources to shift dynamics of racism at the organizational level. In this chapter I first highlight key concepts to help white allies deepen their capacity to create institutional change: white privilege, white culture, and institutional racism. I then offer a model, Multicultural Organizational Development (Jackson, 2005; Jackson & Hardiman, 1994), as a road map to help change agents partner to create inclusive organizations.

Identify White Privilege

A key first step is to develop the capacity to recognize and identify the manifestations of white privilege in our organizations and in our daily lives. I had no concept of what white privilege was for years and scoffed at the term the first time I heard this concept through the work of Dr. Peggy McIntosh and her seminal essay, *"Unpacking the Invisible Knapsack."* Before this, I knew that people of color were discriminated against but had never considered the fact that, as a result, whites were privileged and that I, as a goodhearted, well-intended white person, received undeserved access and benefits that I hadn't earned. It was and still is painful to sit in the reality that I receive a multitude of advantages because people of color are oppressed and denied basic human rights. While it took me many years, I can now often recognize how white privilege operates in my own life as well as the seemingly endless types of advantages whites receive in organizations just because of the color of our skin and how we are raced in this society.

Being considered white comes with a vast number of privileges, including many I have experienced throughout my life. For instance, when I speak in meetings, I am usually assumed to know what I am talking about and my ideas are readily considered while those of my colleagues of color are often questioned and dismissed. When I co-facilitate workshops with a person of color, participants treat me with respect and almost always assume I am the lead trainer. In everyday life, I am given the benefit of the doubt and assumed innocent until my actions prove I have done something wrong or criminal. Even then, I may not be held accountable for any wrong doing. When I interview for a job, I am assumed to be competent and smart until my comments or actions give people reason to think otherwise. Before I was born, my family accumulated more wealth, in part, because my white father had access to the GI Bill from serving in the military in WWII. As a result, he was able to buy a house and complete a graduate degree, whereas veterans of color were most often denied these same benefits. I started out from a very different place in life because of the accumulated advantages my father received due to white privilege and racist practices.

Other white privileges I was oblivious to in organizations include times I've arrived late to a meeting and was not criticized because I was assumed to have been doing something important. I can work in most any organization and feel comfortable in the organizational culture and know I will be successful in the prevailing expectations and practices since white cultural norms are infused into how everything is done, measured, and rewarded.

More than the constant access to mentors, supervisors, leaders, and advisors who look and think like I do, white privilege is also about all the struggles and challenges I DON'T have to experience and the barriers and obstacles I don't face due to my racial identity. I don't have to face the questions and assumptions that I got a job because of my race, even though, in some instances, I believe being white gave me many advantages in the hiring process. I have been assumed competent and completely prepared for a new position or challenge, even though I wasn't. I don't have to endure other daily microaggressions and racist dynamics that people of color experience in the workplace.

In addition, I don't experience the daily racist dynamics that people of color and their loved ones face in society. I do not have to experience racial profiling or live in constant fear that my family members could be killed while interacting with police. I don't have people clutch their purses or wallets tighter or cross the street to avoid me out of fear I am a violent criminal. I don't have people question if I deserve to live in this country or refuse to rent me an apartment or give me respectful customer service just because of the color of my skin.

I don't have to experience any of these exclusionary dynamics and institutional barriers because the culture and climate in almost every organization, as well as many of the policies, practices, programs, and services, are created by whites to benefit whites. I inherited all this access and privilege without doing a thing. White privilege can seem so intangible and invisible that many white people don't realize it is occurring or how they benefit from it. We constantly receive white privilege whether or not we acknowledge it. Even white people who actively work to change racist dynamics in organizations still experience white privilege in the process. When whites speak up, our input is usually valued, and we often get rewarded and appreciated for our leadership and risk-taking.

As long as I denied white privilege, I wasn't able to understand the full power and weight of how it positioned me for success and gave me significant advantages that were denied to people of color. I advanced, moved up, and succeeded on the backs of people of color. I got more because they got far less. The pain of realizing this is overwhelming. It is incredibly painful for me to acknowledge that I received some of my jobs, opportunities, and promotions due to white privilege. I grew up believing in the myth of meritocracy, that if people worked hard, pulled themselves up by their boot straps, they would succeed. In other words, I assumed that success was only dependent on working hard in school and in the workplace and that the game was fair and open for anyone to win. Now, I wasn't totally naïve; I realized that sexism created barriers for women, and heterosexism created obstacles for lesbians, gays, and bisexuals, but I hadn't yet seen the parallel of how racism and white privilege gave whites unearned advantages and benefits that we didn't deserve.

As I deepened my awareness, I felt such guilt and shame. I questioned my competence and skills. Had I gotten this job because I was white and people assumed I was smarter, more capable, and a better leader and employee? When the illusion of meritocracy came crashing down, I felt devastated. It was so difficult to begin to wonder if people liked, respected, and accepted me because I was smart and competent, or because I was white and colluded with white culture and racism. I began to question just about everything in my life.

One aspect of white privilege for me is that I sometimes forget I receive these unearned advantages and privileges and begin to expect them as rights that I deserve. For example, when I do not get preferential treatment by a customer service representative or if I have to wait in a long line at the post office just like the people of color ahead of me, or if the cable technician is late or doesn't show up, I can get angry. I'm not just a little irritated but am frustrated that I didn't receive the level of treatment to which I felt entitled. In a voice oozing with arrogance and self-righteousness, I have demanded better service, to be treated like I deserve, as a privileged, superior white person in this world. To be fair, I am usually completely unconscious and unaware of how I am reacting out of white privilege. Yet, whether I recognize it in the moment or not, my negative, racist impact still exists.

Understand White Culture

I can't count how many times I have thought or heard other whites say, "It's boring being white. We don't have a culture like people of color do." In reality, white people have a very definitive culture that is so powerful and pervasive that it is often invisible to most of us, possibly even to many people of color. White cultural norms are deeply embedded in the daily practices, policies, programs, and services of almost every organization with which I have worked or consulted. It is hard to recognize because most of us have been taught and still believe that white culture is normal and reflects good business practices, when in reality it can erode morale, productivity, and teamwork for people of color and also for most white employees. While white people still benefit from white privilege and white cultural norms in organizations, we are also hurt by them and would greatly benefit from partnering with colleagues of color to create more inclusive organizational practices.

We can see white culture operating in how we define professional. In most predominantly white organizations, employees are expected to adhere to mostly unwritten rules of professional behavior. These rules, in part, reflect whiteness in how they value and privilege people who dress a certain way, wear their hair in specific styles, and are overly polite and unemotional in their styles of communication. Employees are rewarded for avoiding direct conflict and using indirect communication. To be valued and have their ideas considered, most people have to express themselves in a very impersonal, monotonous, and soft-spoken approach and offer their ideas in a very concise, analytical, rational, and linear way. If anyone wants to offer a somewhat different perspective, they have to downplay their ideas in a diminutive, undemonstrative, and low key way or they may be accused of being disruptive and creating too much conflict in the workplace.

While these implicit white cultural norms are enforced for employees in the middle and lower levels of many organizations, many white leaders and other contributors considered to be particularly valuable are often exempt from having to fit into these constrictive white cultural codes of conduct. I have heard multiple stories of senior white leaders who have raised their voices to end conversations, slammed their fists on the table, and aggressively interrupted others to push their points without being held accountable. In fact, they may be praised as strong leaders. However, if leaders of color try to use these same tactics, they are most likely challenged and criticized if not punished for these very same behaviors.

I am deeply grateful to the work of Tema Okun for the essay, "White Supremacy Culture" (Okun, 2001). In the article, Okun describes fifteen key patterns of white culture that can have a negative impact on many employees in the workplace, including perfectionism, a sense of urgency, objectivity, only one right way, worship of the written word, defensiveness, the right to comfort, paternalism, either-or thinking, quantity over quality, fear of open conflict, power hoarding, and individualism. These cultural norms and practices have become the unquestioned standard in most organizations. It can be difficult to notice these white cultural practices since they have become so readily accepted as valuable and critical to organizational success.

Okun (2001) describes antidotes to each of these core aspects of white culture. For instance, instead of insisting there is only one right way and getting defensive when employees raise issues, leaders can create a collaborative decision-making process to empower all employees to offer creative ideas and solutions to solve complex problems.

Instead of isolating or reprimanding those who challenge or question the status quo, organizations can create structures that invite and reward continuous improvement and efforts to innovate. For a more in-depth understanding of these critical concepts, I highly recommend you review this outstanding, insightful article and explore how your organization reflects these white cultural norms and practices and which antidotes may be useful to consider.

http://www.dismantlingracism.org/uploads/4/3/5/7/43579015/whitesupcul13.pdf.

Unfortunately, in many organizations, employees who try to challenge these white cultural norms or shift these exclusive dynamics may risk their reputation or future promotions. I believe the long-term success of any organization depends on the ability to re-engineer white cultural climates to create more inclusive, innovative, and collaborative environments where all people can thrive and contribute to their fullest potential.

This change process can start with each of us as individuals. I used to collude and replicate many of these white cultural norms without ever questioning their usefulness or validity. Over time I have come to reject the idea that this is the only way that organizations can be successful. I try to create a very different climate and culture in my workshops and coaching sessions.

It takes intentional, enlightened leadership to create work environments where all employees are empowered to question traditional white cultural practices and develop a climate that supports the success of all employees. A more inclusive, multicultural organization can promote engaged, authentic dialogue and disagreement at all levels of the organization where leaders consistently invite feedback and innovative ideas that may challenge the status quo. In addition, in thriving multicultural organizations, employees are encouraged to take risks and if things don't work as planned, then lessons-learned conversations help everyone identify what worked well and what could be done differently to create greater success in the future. In this type of learning environment, employees are rewarded for building meaningful partnerships across silos and hierarchical levels to spark the best ideas and most productive collaborations. Unfortunately, the vast majority of the institutions I am familiar with are far from achieving this type of work culture.

Continuing to operate within these unexamined white cultural practices can undermine the capacity to achieve organizational strategic goals and create a toxic workplace environment for everyone, with additional negative impact for people of color. It takes great courage to speak up and challenge these ingrained white cultural norms. There could be significant risk for challenging the status quo and working to create a more culturally inclusive work environment. Yet if we don't, we slowly lose a piece of ourselves each and every day we stay in these oppressive organizations.

Identify Institutional Racism

Institutional racism manifests when racist stereotypes and white cultural practices are embedded into organizational policies, practices, and infrastructures. Institutional racism is insidious and invisible to most whites. Even when we recognize these practices and policies, we can feel overwhelmed and incompetent to know how to begin to change them. Recognizing interpersonal microaggressions is not enough. To create inclusive, racially just organizations, we must consistently recognize and interrupt institutional racism in all of its forms. The challenge is that these racist dynamics have become so commonplace that most whites never question them.

Hiring practices were the most frequently cited examples of institutional racism in a survey I sent out to white change agents. Racist dynamics permeate most every aspect of traditional searches and continue to privilege whites at every step of the process, including who gets chosen to serve on Search Committees, how they are often ill-prepared to interrupt implicit racist bias, the required qualifications and experiences for a position, how positions are advertised, the formal and informal criteria used to review resumes and portfolios, and the process used to select candidates to interview. In addition, the interview process itself often provides greater comfort and ease for white candidates while many people of color experience a distinct chill in the room as they participate in interviews and open forums.

Most hiring practices institutionalize white cultural standards for what is considered effective leadership, conflict management, communication, appearance, research, and presentation styles. Discussions about the top white candidates are often fraught with coded racist phrases such as, "He would be a good fit," "She seems like a team player," and "He went to a good school." In contrast, the credentials and competence of candidates of color are often questioned with other racially coded phrases, including, "I don't know if their work experience is what we are looking for," "I'm not sure their style will work with our customers," "I think they would be great for our organization, but I don't think this is the right job for them," and "Their research is somewhat on the periphery of the field."

Another all too common racist dynamic colleagues report is someone saying, "Don't get me wrong, I support diversity; but we don't want to lower our standards just to make a diverse hire." Most, if not all, of these racist comments and practices go unaddressed in the vast majority of search processes I know about. And organizations continue to hire more white people and bemoan the fact they can't find any "qualified minorities," another racist term that often goes unchallenged.

There are some proven approaches to minimize the rampant implicit racism in search processes, including having a clear set of relevant competencies and demonstrated capacities that guide the review of applications, interview questions, and selection discussions and decisions; requiring intensive

Search Committee trainings that explicitly address issues of implicit bias; assigning a Search Advocate to each committee who has a demonstrated capacity to help teams run inclusive search processes and interrupt racist dynamics that occur; and having a senior leader and HR manager review and sign-off on all recommended pools for interviews as well as the list of final candidates.

However, all of the best practices are only as useful as the people who try to implement them. Regular training and accountability structures are essential elements for any inclusive hiring process.

Another predictable pitfall in the hiring process that creates racist dynamics throughout the organization involves the persistent practice of using hiring to only change the racial demographics in the organization, instead of also emphasizing the need to increase the cultural competencies of all leaders and employees. As long as the only focus is on hiring more people of color, without a parallel goal of ensuring that every person hired is culturally competent, the pattern will continue of hiring whites without the necessary skills and capacity to work effectively on racially diverse teams or to serve the increasingly diverse customer populations. The outcome of this insidious practice continues to place the responsibility of creating greater inclusion on the few people of color in the organization while letting white leaders and employees off the hook for doing their part.

Most people of color I have met describe having to "work two jobs for one paycheck" as they are frequently assigned to committees, task forces, and search committees to make them more "diverse," while their white counterparts are not tasked with these extra burdens and, as a result, can focus on their primary job responsibilities. In addition, professionals of color may be called away from their regular job responsibilities to do community outreach and recruiting or to work with current or potential customers of color because the white professionals responsible for these relationships do not have the cultural competence to engage effectively. Middle level and upper level leaders of color are often sought out as mentors and coaches by employees of color who are supervised by white people who don't have the competence to support their professional growth and development of the staff of color they supervise. These added responsibilities consume a lot of mental and physical energy for the very few people of color in leadership.

Some organizations are experiencing greater success because they have institutionalized their commitment to require that all final candidates, across racial identity, must demonstrate the cultural competence to work effectively in a multicultural organization as well as the capacity to create inclusive policies, practices, programs, and services that meet the needs of the full customer base. In short, every white person as well as every person of color that is hired must be culturally competent.

While trying to identify the seemingly endless examples of institutional racism is beyond the scope of this book, I want to highlight a few more common dynamics. Informal and inadequate onboarding and orientation practices result in whites receiving far more information from their white peers and colleagues about how to be successful in the organization including access to the unwritten rules of performance. New employees of color may be fortunate to get this same level of coaching if there are enough other people of color with whom they interact or if their white managers are competent at supervising across race.

Many performance management systems are so subjective and loosely monitored that it is common that racial bias influences how managers evaluate employees through a lens of white cultural norms, resulting in white employees receiving higher rankings than people of color. Given that the vast majority of middle and senior leaders are white in most organizations, coupled with the tendency to coach and mentor people with whom we are more comfortable, many employees of color do not receive the critical informal mentoring and sponsorship for success. These types of support and supervision are influential in both promotional practices and additional assignments that provide stretch opportunities which can put an employee on the fast track.

Many more institutionalized racist practices result in some very common dynamics I see in organizations, such as whites consistently getting promoted over the people of color who trained them, white employees going over the heads of their supervisors of color to work directly with a white senior leader, and employees of color considered more of a potential liability than a valued resource. These are just some of the examples that influence who is successful in organizations, whose voice is valued, who ascends to leadership, and who develops and enforces policies and practices. Taken together, these are the types of institutional racist dynamics that maintain the status quo in most predominantly white organizations.

Some individual leaders can make meaningful changes to dismantle institutional racism in their spheres of influence. However, without an organization-wide strategic plan and a system of accountability to ensure sustainability, any of these modifications at the micro-level can be undone by the next leader. Shifting institutional racism and white cultural practices requires significant organizational culture change. Many leaders have found the model, Multicultural Organizational Development (Jackson & Hardiman, 1994) a useful strategic road map to envision and implement this level of transformation.

Multicultural Organizational Development (MCOD)

I have consulted with a number of organizations that have used the Jackson & Hardiman six-stage MCOD model to help leaders and employees learn a common set of concepts and terms and to use race as a lens as they engage in authentic, meaningful discussions about the current organizational culture and climate. In these conversations, members of the organization identify their vision of a racially just organization, develop a shared understanding of the current state, and begin to recognize the reality of the gap between where they are and where they hope to be. Facilitating these sessions with a significant cross section of members of the organization can generate a lot of energy and passion as well as mobilize leaders and employees to work together to create more racially just organizations.

Most organizations seem to have a change process that is haphazard, unplanned, and incremental as well as one that is often hastily formed in reaction to the most recent crisis or negative headline (Harper, 2011; Marchesani & Jackson, 2005; Obear & Kerr, 2015). What is needed instead is a strategic, thoughtful plan to guide long-term culture change efforts to create sustainable, meaningful inclusion and racial justice. The Multicultural Organizational Development (MCOD) model (Jackson, 2005; Jackson & Hardiman, 1994) provides a useful framework to help leaders identify any cultural or structural inequities as well as dynamics of institutional racism so they can develop interventions and change processes to create more racially inclusive organizations.

Once leaders and employees understand the six stages of the MCOD model they can discuss and identify which stage best describes the current state of their organization. There are three different levels of organizations in the model: Monocultural, Non-Discriminating, and Multicultural

Jackson/Hardiman MCOD Continuum

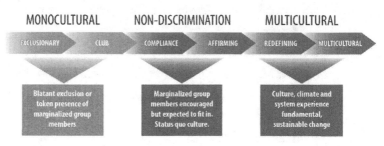

Jackson 2005; Graphic developd by Dr. Shelly Kerr

Leaders in Monocultural Organizations have no interest in becoming a Multicultural Organization and exert effort, possibly unconsciously, to maintain the status and privilege of the whites who hold power (Jackson & Holvino, 1988; Obear & Kerr, 2015). At both Stage 1, The Exclusionary Organization, and Stage 2, The Club Organization, white cultural norms and practices are designed to openly maintain the power and dominance of whites while the few people of color in the organization may experience hostility and racial harassment that go unaddressed. The policies of a Club organization may not be as explicit about excluding people of color, but the racist impact of the culture and climate is similar to that of an Exclusionary Organization.

In Non-Discriminating Organizations, there is some interest in hiring more people of color, particularly at the lower levels of the organization, as long as they assimilate into the white cultural norms and practices (Jackson & Holvino, 1988) and improve the organizational reputation as an inclusive place to work. In a Stage 3 Compliance Organization leaders focus on complying with any external regulations or federal laws and work to present an inclusive, though inaccurate, image through their written policies and public face. People of color may be hired as leaders in pockets of the organization but are often treated as tokens within the management ranks. While there is more active recruiting of people of color in a Stage 4 Affirming Organization and a commitment to eliminate discriminatory practices, employees of color are still expected to fit into the white cultural norms (Jackson & Holvino, 1988).

In Multicultural Organizations at Stages 5 and 6, all employees are trained, empowered, and held accountable for continuously reviewing and revising current policies, practices, programs, and services to meet the needs of both whites and people of color. In addition, if they ever identify any unintended negative impact on people of color that creates barriers to access or success, employees are expected to quickly shift these practices to create greater equity and inclusion. In Multicultural Organizations, it is everyone's responsibility to create racial justice and inclusion in everything they do (Jackson & Holvino, 1988).

In the list of recommended Further Readings at the end of the book there is a citation for a chapter I co-wrote exploring how one university division used the MCOD model to facilitate significant cultural change in their organization (Obear & Kerr, 2015). Common strategic actions in a long-term culture change process include deepening the capacity of leaders and internal change teams; assessing organizational readiness and the current stage of development; analyzing current programs, policies, services, and practices; designing and implementing a plan for continuous improvement; and ensuring progress with a meaningful system of accountability (Jackson, 2005).

Creating greater racial justice through sustainable, meaningful organizational change requires that white leaders and change agents effectively partner with people of color and stay true to their vision as they navigate and resolve the inevitable stiff resistance they will face. This long-term culture change process requires significant courage, stamina, patience, and resilient leadership (Obear & Kerr, 2015). It is difficult, challenging work, but I know no other path to create racially just organizations.

All of our learning, reflections, and preparations as white allies are necessary but not always sufficient to help us respond effectively in difficult situations. There will still be times we come up short and don't know what to say or what to do. In the next chapter, I highlight ways I have responded to some of the challenging moments I have experienced as a white change agent.

CHAPTER 7
RESPONDING TO
RACIST SITUATIONS

I started to feel uneasy in a meeting as I watched three different white people challenge the leader of color. I was just visiting this organization and knew the leader and one other person of color in the room, but I didn't know the full of the context of the conversation. I wanted the dynamics to shift but didn't feel it was my place to say anything.

Afterwards, I shared my concerns about the race dynamics I had noticed with my colleague of color who simply asked, "Why didn't you say something?" I felt embarrassed and incompetent, and I knew she was right that I should have said something. A whirlwind of perfectly logical explanations swirled in my mind: I'm not a member of this group, they wouldn't have taken me seriously, and my comments wouldn't have made a difference anyway. As I dug beneath those excuses, I found some deeper intrapersonal roots and fears, including: What if I made a mistake? What if I made it worse? What would people think of me? I might look foolish, and people will realize I am not as competent as they think I am. The truth is, my silence was a clear indicator of my degree of competence.

When I feel caught off-guard or experience a new type of racist situation, I often freeze and believe I don't know what to do. I feel triggered, and all the tools I know and teach seem to disappear from my toolkit. As I look back, I now see I could have easily said, "Excuse me, I know I may not have all of the context of what's happening right now, but I am feeling increasingly uncomfortable with the tone of this conversation." And then I could have waited to see what happened next as I took multiple deep breaths!

I wish there were a comprehensive checklist of what to do in every type of circumstance. Once I have seen or thought through a specific situation, I feel much more confident and skilled if I experience similar racist dynamics in the future. But how do I get prepared to react to new types of situations?

In reality, there are many tools and concepts that can help me decide how to engage and, if I am centered and grounded enough, I most often respond effectively enough to start a conversation. Over the years, it has been helpful to observe other white people respond in difficult situations as well as to talk through some scenarios with mentors and colleagues. In the following sections, I share some of my current thoughts and approaches to engaging a wide variety of common racist dynamics that are challenging for many of my clients and workshop participants with whom I work. I believe there may be multiple useful ways to respond in any given racist situation. I offer these ideas as possibilities to consider. My hope is that you find a few more tools and techniques to add to your toolkit.

Why We Don't Speak Up

Before I offer clients specific tools and strategies to respond in difficult situations, I first talk with them about the reasons they choose to not speak up in those moments. See if you can relate to some of these additional common fears. I know I have felt them all!

Are you concerned if you confront other white people that they will get angry and come after you? Or hold a grudge and find ways to retaliate and undermine you in the future? Are you afraid of damaging your relationships with other whites, including your friends or your supervisor? Are you concerned you'll be "thrown out of the club" and lose access to information, resources, and power-brokers? Are you afraid of what white people will think of you and how they might ruin your reputation? Do you fear future career opportunities may be sabotaged if people begin to think of you as a trouble-maker, too outspoken, too aggressive, or not a team player?

There are realistic costs for speaking up, ones that our colleagues of color have been experiencing all their lives. The Old White's Club is powerful and well networked in our organizations and often nationally as well. While I can feel overwhelmed with these fears, they also help me ground my responses in the larger context and help me be more strategic and, hopefully, more effective in the long-term.

One way to increase the possibility that our questions and comments will be considered and not dismissed outright is to invest time and energy into building more meaningful relationships with key white colleagues and leaders in our organizations. Instead of judging and dismissing those you believe "don't get it," these colleagues might be exactly the white people with whom you need to develop a relationship. Spend time learning what they care about, what motivates them, and how they positively contribute to the success of the organization. Most white people are far more willing, in my experience, to tolerate challenges from people they like and with whom they already have a working relationship. Plant the seeds now and water them with care so you can harvest good will and the benefit of the doubt when you need them in the future.

But What If This Happens?

Intent vs. Impact

I remember a time in a workshop when a white participant was confronted on their comment, and their immediate triggered reaction was, "That wasn't my intent!" I responded by saying, "I rarely consciously intend the negative impact of the comments I make. I'm open to exploring your intent in a moment, but I wonder if you can first acknowledge what you heard Alisha say was the impact of your comment?" Another approach I have used when white people seem to only focus on their intent is to say, "I trust you didn't intend this. And I hope you can also realize the impact was very different than what you consciously intended."

It has also been useful for me to talk about implicit bias as well by sharing, "There are many stories I could tell you of racist comments I have made and I would have sworn I hadn't intended any negative impact. And the truth is, when I got honest with myself and dug underneath my comment or action, I most often realized that some racist implicit bias and stereotypes were fueling my reaction. I wasn't aware at that time, but unconsciously, just below the surface, these racist beliefs shaped my response. Can you relate at all?"

A related situation I often see is how white people will come to the rescue of another colleague who was confronted about her racist comment or behavior. It can sound like, "Oh, Kelly didn't mean it. She was just joking. She isn't racist. Her best friend is Latina. She is just having a tough time at work lately." In this case, I might respond by saying, "I know she is a good person. Most of us are and we can still make racist comments that have a negative impact. The fact that she is a well-intended colleague has me hopeful that she will care about her unintended impact and want to stay in the conversation to better understand what happened."

Shifting the focus to our marginalized identity(s)
Another common dynamic I see in every white caucus or workshop I facilitate on racism is how some white people tend to shift the focus of the conversation away from whiteness and race and begin talking about one of their marginalized identities. The most common examples I

experience occur when women talk about experiencing sexism or sexual violence, people who grew up poor or working class talk about the pain of classism in their lives, and people who identify as lesbian, gay, or bisexual share the anguish and fear of facing homophobia and heterosexism in their organization and in society. I have used this tactic myself, focusing on my marginalized identities to avoid feeling the pain and discomfort of the realities of racism and my role in perpetuating the status quo from my white privilege. While whites with intersecting identities in marginalized groups may experience white privilege somewhat differently from those with few, if any, marginalized groups, I believe it is critical that whites initially complete significant self-work and healing focused solely on racism and internalized dominance before they explore the nuances associated with their intersecting marginalized identities.

In these situations where whites have shifted to focus on a marginalized experience, I have often said, "I notice you just shifted the conversation to talk about being gay. Did you notice? Can you say more about why you moved away from talking about race?" Another approach I have used is to acknowledge the pain of the person's marginalized experience before I refocus the conversation back onto race, "I can't imagine what that must have been like. I am so sorry you experienced that. My guess is the pain and anger you feel may be a window to understand what many people of color may be feeling from the persistent violence of racism in their lives. As you heard all the stories we have been sharing about the ways we as white people have colluded and actively participated in racist dynamics, what could you relate to?"

Occasionally, participants will continue to talk about their marginalized identity, and I may choose to be more direct in my response, "I notice this is the second time you have brought up an example of growing up in poverty. I know when I continue to refocus on my marginalized identities it is because I am often feeling very uncomfortable looking at all the white privilege I receive as well as the horrific emotional and physical violence people of color experience every day. Can you say more about what you are feeling right now as I nudge you to keep the focus on race?" Usually this approach will open the door to the deeper levels of resistance. The gift is that many more white people in the room are thinking and feeling similar thoughts as this participant, and we now have the chance to engage them openly.

Blame the messenger

After being confronted by a person of color, I have seen whites seek support from each other by complaining about the way in which the person of color gave the feedback. I have done this to avoid having to consider and sit with the impact my actions had on others. This avoidance tactic can sound like, "I can't believe she was so aggressive when she attacked you! That wasn't very professional." When I notice this defense strategy I often respond with, "I actually experienced her very differently. I thought she was clear and direct in her comments, and not at all aggressive. I have sometimes accused a person of color of attacking me when they were only taking the risk to share some feedback with me. In the past, I have felt angry when people of color have confronted me and focused more on how they engaged me than on what they were trying to help me realize about myself. Some people call this 'tone-policing'. Have you heard about this concept?" After they respond to me, I may go in a number of directions including, "I know it is hard for me to accept critical feedback. I hate knowing that my actions may have been harmful to others. I understand the feedback she gave you because I have received similar feedback from others about my actions. If you want to talk more, I would be glad to sit with you for a while."

In each of the previous examples you may notice how I use the various tools in PAIRS™, the skill set I described in more detail in Chapter 3. You may want to review that section or the materials on my website, www.drkathyobear.com/racebook, to better recognize how I use these tools in the following examples.

We are all one race
In workshops, I have recently heard several white people say something like, "I hate that you call me 'white!' Why do you have to use all those terms like black and Hispanic and Asian? We are all one race, the human race!"

In order to find a way to acknowledge and join them before I offer an alternative perspective I may ask, "Can you say more about what you value about all of us being the human race and what we all deserve as human beings?" As they share more, I can usually find something to build on as I continue, "I agree that as humans we all deserve to be respected and treated with dignity. And I share your vision of a world where we can all be seen as the brilliant, lovable individuals we are."

At this point, I tend to turn to the whole group and ask a rhetorical question such as, "Who else wants a world where we all are valued, respected and can contribute to our full potential?" Usually most participants raise their hands to agree. Then I pivot as I respond back to the original participant, "My guess is you can see that we aren't fully there yet. As much as you may treat everyone with respect and dignity, regardless of their race, every day I hear about or see whites making racist assumptions and treating people of color negatively. Do you sometimes see that as well?" As they tend to nod, I continue, "So until all people of color get the same equitable treatment as I do, I will keep holding your vision of the world that I believe is possible, and I will continue to talk about the daily indignities and micro-aggressions that people of color experience every day. Any reaction to what I am saying?"

People of color are racist, too!
Another challenging situation is how white people try to deflect attention away from their behaviors by saying, "People of color are racist, too! Last week I heard someone in the office say they hated white people!" I might enter by asking, "How did you feel when you heard that? I might

have felt a bit put-off by that comment and been worried they were talking about me."

Depending on their reaction, I might say, "Over the years, I have heard some people of color make prejudiced comments about whites, and they were sometimes hard to hear. I found that when I stayed in the conversation and asked them how they were doing or why they felt that way, they usually started to tell me about some recent, really painful racist situations they experienced or that happened to members of their family. And I could better understand the depth of their anger and frustration. And it made me realize how rarely I hear negative comments about white people compared to how much more frequently I see and hear stereotypic and racist comments about people of color. Can you relate at all?"

I may then move on by saying, "And we're talking about how any of us, white, Latinx, Asian American, Black, Native American, Middle Eastern, and Multiracial, we can all have assumptions and stereotypes about other racial groups. These are painful. Anybody can have and act on their prejudices. However, it's my understanding that the term racism is talking more about the way these prejudices have been used to create organizations and institutions that privilege whites at the expense of people of color. I remember the first time I heard this definition in a workshop: Racism is privilege plus power. People of color can react out of their prejudice; they don't have the power or privilege to institutionalize racism in daily practices, policies, and services. This may not make sense. It took me quite a while to shift my thinking. But if you want to talk more, my door is always open."

I don't want you to get the impression that I easily respond to these types of questions all the time. I often feel triggered and thrown off-balance by some of these comments, which is why I often start by asking a question so I get a moment to re-center myself before I open my mouth.

We are post-racial

A type of comment that often gets under my skin is when white people say, "All this focus on race only makes things worse. We are post-racial now. I mean, we elected a black president and we have hired so many people of color recently. Affirmative Action worked, but now it's not needed anymore. Whites will be a minority soon and we already are in many states. Why can't you move past this and focus on more important issues?"

It's that last comment that is particularly triggering as I imagine their next comment to be, "What more do those people of color want?!?!" After I take a few deep breaths and try hard to remember when I have thought or said something similar, I can usually de-escalate my emotions enough to say something useful. I might enter with, "I wish I could agree with you. I so wish that race didn't matter any- more. And I wish that Affirmative Action had successfully achieved its goal, but I recently saw another statistic that again pointed out how white women, by far, have been the beneficiaries of Affirmative Action practices. And while we do see some progress with hiring people of color into leadership roles, even if you look at the top leaders at our peer institutions or in the government, they are still mostly white as are most of their direct reports. I'm curious what others think?"

You may have noticed that I didn't start off with a question or by relating in on this one. Sometimes I do share statistics, research, or other patterns as a way to embolden some white participants to join me and speak up. If I had been a little less triggered, I might have entered differently, and yet I think this type of approach can also be very useful, if used only occasionally. If I find myself in the "telling" mode more than a few times in a meeting or a training session, I try to back off and invite others to become more engaged. I believe more effective learning happens when we engage with our peers and people we know and respect. I believe my role, as a colleague or a facilitator, is to model how whites can engage more productively and create the container for greater courage among group members.

Racist jokes
Many white people tell me they struggle with how to respond when a colleague or family member makes a racist comment or "joke". Sometimes I simply try to use humor by saying, "You did not just say that?!" I often start with a lighter tone to give them a chance to reflect on what they just said. Often, people quickly apologize for their comment without my having to say much more. The challenge is that while they may now realize what they said crossed

a line, they may not yet understand why. I might then ask, "What do you think the impact is when you say that?" Or say, "I've said that before without realizing the negative racist impact I was having." And then I would continue to share more about the impact. Another approach I have used is to ask, "Help me understand more about what you mean?" or "I'm curious when you first heard that term or phrase?"

Sometimes, I ask a question to clarify what I think they said, "I want to make sure I understand your point. Are you saying that..." Usually they recognize the impact of their comment and begin to backtrack or acknowledge they crossed a line.

Unfortunately, some white people may need a far more direct and confrontational approach before they change their behavior. Other ways I have responded include, "What were you intending to communicate with that remark?" Or "My guess is you don't know how offensive that comment is to me and others." At some point, if this occurs in the workplace, I frame the conversation within the organizational context by saying, "Whether we know it or not, these types of disrespectful comments hurt our team dynamics and create a stressful, toxic work environment. I'm glad to talk with you more about this."

This place is too politically correct

A related situation occurs when people say, "We have gotten way too politically correct around here! You gotta look out for the PC police!" In response, I usually ask a question to get them to talk more, "What do you mean?" Their common response often is, "You can't say anything anymore!" To which I might call their bluff by asking, "What do you want to be able to say?" If they list off a few things they want to be able to say, then I can explore the negative impact of these on our colleagues and me. To bring some closure I may say, "As employees in any organization, we all have to be thoughtful about what we say and try to engage in ways that recognizes the value of each person. I want to work in an inclusive environment where we treat each other with respect and dignity, and we work together to help our clients. My guess is that is important to you as well. If you ever want to talk more, let's grab some coffee sometime."

As a rule, I think it is good practice to check back in with the white people I have confronted later that day or the next morning. I don't usually ask directly about the previous conversation, but I stop by their office or send an email about something else to show them I am moving forward and still in relationship with them.

Workplace gossip
It is particularly painful for me to write about this next racist dynamic because I did this so many times and deeply regret the harm I caused through my actions. How many times have you heard whites make negative remarks to each other about people of color with whom they work but never talk directly to people of color about their concerns?

This form of workplace gossip is damaging on several levels. If people are like me, I never talked directly to my colleagues of color about my observations or frustrations about them in the same way that I would engage white colleagues with whom I had a concern. By not engaging in a conversation with a colleague of color about an issue I had about our work together, I was avoiding any possibility of conflict or being seen as racist. I also denied my colleagues of color the opportunity to consider and discuss my feedback. Depending on how I approached the situation, it could be my observations might have helped them be more successful in the organization. Additionally, by only focusing on their behavior, I avoided examining how or if my racist assumptions and stereotypes were fueling my negative judgments towards my colleague of color. I continued to operate out of denial and fear without realizing how my actions and inactions were negatively impacting others.

Today, if I hear whites sharing negative feedback among themselves about people of color I ask, "What did they say when you talked to them about it?" Most often, just like me, they hadn't talked with their colleague. I might continue with a few questions, including, "What specific behaviors are you concerned about? How did you make meaning of what they said or did? What could be other ways to interpret what they did? Have you ever seen any white colleagues do similar behaviors? If so, what was your reaction and did you talk directly with them? Do you hold white colleagues to the same level of expected performance as you do colleagues of color?"

At some point, I would definitely relate in and share my own fears and concerns about engaging in authentic dialogue about my expectations and perceptions of performance with people of color. I might also tell a story of how I realized my racist stereotypes clouded my perception and interpretation of my colleague of color's actions and times I gave my white colleagues the benefit of doubt. I might end the conversation by saying, "It may not be useful, but I am more than happy to talk with you about ways to approach this colleague. I know it has been helpful to me to talk things through before I give someone feedback, especially if I am feeling nervous or unsure. Glad to grab lunch sometime."

Here is an example of how I used many of the types of questions and tools I just described. While coaching a white client, she talked about her frustration with a person of color who had missed an important deadline. As we dug around for the intrapersonal roots and possible judgments fueling her emotions, she admitted that she saw her colleague as unprofessional and lazy. As we talked further, she began to recognize how she was upholding the white cultural norms of immediacy, perfectionism, and urgency. When I asked her how she has reacted when white colleagues missed a deadline, she paused and with a clearer tone of humility, acknowledged that she had felt more empathy for them, asked more about the challenges they were facing, and extended the deadline around their needs. As I asked her more questions, she said she had taken the time to support and problem-solve with a white colleague, who also happened to be a friend of hers. And she reflected that she really didn't know her colleague of color as well, and when she missed the deadline, she didn't follow-up to see how the colleague doing or how she might support her.

As painful as it was for this client, she had a significant breakthrough in that conversation as she realized how often she reached out and built relationships with her white colleagues, and yet how little time or attention she invested into her colleagues of color. As she explored the initial incident in this larger context, she saw how her fear of being called racist had contributed to her not developing enough of a relationship with this colleague of color to treat her with the same level of respect and flexibility that she gave to her white colleagues.

When I lead white caucuses or provide one-on-one coaching with white leaders, I find that participants have the space to do the self-work I have described throughout this book. In these settings, white people have the opportunity to honestly explore the depths of their racist stereotypes and behaviors, identify new ways to engage others, and shift their internalized racist beliefs. This space is important for white people to develop their capacity to address racism and become more effective leaders. White-on-white anti-racism work can be found in a variety of settings. I hope you seek out these spaces and give yourself this gift of personal development.

Choose Your Intentions Wisely

A critical aspect of responding effectively is being grounded in positive, productive intentions. I have said all the right words at times, but my tone, energy, and non-verbal communication were clear clues that my actions were fueled by negative, unproductive intentions. As a result, the interactions usually did not go very well.

Have you ever engaged a person of color in an attempt to prove you were not racist or to get them to approve of your efforts as a white ally? Or have you ever spoken up in a meeting to try to smooth over conflict or to claim the title of "the good white" in the room?

I have reacted out of all of these unproductive intentions as well as many more that fueled my ineffective interactions with white people, including wanting to be seen as the most competent white person in the room; aiming to "take out" whites who say something racist; and trying to win the argument that proves I am right and other white people are wrong.

None of these, usually unconscious, intentions help me facilitate greater connection, understanding, or meaningful change. All I accomplish when my actions are rooted in these intentions is to shame other whites, create greater distance among us, and lose the opportunity to support our development as white allies.

Before we begin to engage others, it is critical that we first get clear about our conscious and unconscious intentions.

People will energetically feel our intentions and often react to us before we even open our mouths. I am far more effective when I am grounded in more productive intentions, including: meet people where they are; relate in and connect; treat others with respect and dignity; leave no one behind; do no harm; leave people feeling whole; and model the behaviors and values I espouse.

There are many more racist dynamics that I and other white people, including myself, continue to perpetuate that could fill many more chapters! I believe we will always encounter racist situations we may not have seen before. The more I keep learning and continually practice effective responses, the more confidence and presence I have in these unexpected moments.

I hope the scenarios and reflections in this chapter give you a few more tools to interrupt racist comments and possibly help whites deepen their understanding and shift their behaviors. We make a difference every time we speak up. We either collude and perpetuate racism or take a stand for racial justice. The difference we make is up to us.

CHAPTER 8
CONCLUSION

"Life doesn't allow for us to go back and fix what we have done wrong in the past, but it does allow for us to live each day better than our last."
- Unknown Author

I was leading a large group discussion when a participant of color publicly confronted me saying that I had made a racist comment to her at the break. I immediately felt terrified that she had called me racist. My mind was swirling with fearful, de-stabilizing thoughts: "What did I do wrong? I really blew it! What will people think of me? I've completely lost all credibility and respect as a white ally. And what do I do now?" Somehow, I was able stay present enough to say, "I apologize for my comment and am open to hearing more about the impact I had on you." I was shaking in my boots, on high alert, and just waiting for the next revelation that I was a horrible racist and a complete fraud. I had practiced dialogue skills enough to acknowledge her feelings even as I felt so deeply triggered and off-balance. As I listened, I tried to take deep breaths and shift my negative thoughts by using these statements as mantras: "Stay focused. Own the impact. Stay open to the learning. Everything happens for a reason."

After she shared her experience, I paraphrased back what I heard about the impact of my behavior. I could tell by her face I didn't fully get it right and paused as she clarified what I missed. I felt even more defeated but took a breath as I summarized the additional pieces I had overlooked. As she nodded, which I took to mean I more fully understood the situation, I said something like, "I regret what I said and the painful impact I had on you. I intend to keep exploring what I did so I can uncover and shift the racist attitudes and lack of knowledge that fueled my comment. I commit to doing my self-work so I can show up differently in the future."

Still feeling shaky, I paused to see if she wanted to say anything more. When she didn't, I then broadened my focus to the full group and opened up the conversation for others to share how they were impacted by this interaction. At the next break, I intentionally walked by her and nodded as I slowly passed by. I didn't want to force an interaction in case she didn't want to engage me at that moment, and I also wanted to put myself in the position to continue the conversation if she wanted to follow-up. She didn't, so I kept moving.

This was one of the most challenging and difficult moments I have facilitated. I felt triggered and unsteady for at least another hour as we continued the training. I had to use most every stress-releasing and re-centering tool I knew to stay present and, hopefully, be somewhat useful the rest of that day.

After the session, I called a couple of white colleagues to process the situation. I am deeply grateful for whites who are willing to give me honest feedback, relate in, and offer insights for how I can move forward on my journey. I might not be able to stay in this work without their support.

Later that night, I thought about my experience at the EYCA Development Lab and wondered if I would have had the capacity to show up earlier that day if I hadn't been willing to change based on the feedback I got back in the late 1990's. Maybe everything does happen for a reason, or at least we can turn every difficult moment into a powerful opportunity for our own growth and development.

What If They Call Me Racist?

"As we let our light shine, we unconsciously give other people permission to do the same. As we are liberated from our own fear, our presence actually liberates others."
- Marianne Williamson

I still believe that one of our deepest fears as white people is to be called racist by a person of color. If we can move through this fear, we will be much more effective as change agents as we partner to create racial justice. If we don't, we will continue to perpetuate the racist status quo.

I have seen many white people stop out and drop out of this work just like I did. We obsess and wallow in fear, guilt, and shame as we try to figure out what we did wrong so we won't get called out again. But we are wasting our time and energy on the wrong goal.

Instead, we need to develop the capacity to pause and acknowledge the negative impact of our comments and behaviors and accept the reality that we still harbor and react out of racist implicit bias. We need to develop the ability to stay open to the learning and transformative healing that can happen in these moments, however painful they may be.

I never want any racial prejudice to fuel my actions and cause further pain, angst, or harm to people of color. And when I react in ways that perpetuate racist dynamics, I want to be engaged by others so I can do my self-work to explore what I did as well as what I was thinking and feeling in the moment. I want to learn from the experience so I show up a more effective change agent for racial justice in the future.

In my experience, when I have chosen to stay in the conversation to explore and feel the impact of my actions, my relationships with people of color have deepened and strengthened. Maybe they began to trust that I won't get aggressive or too defensive, but instead, will stay open to the learning and the lesson as I act on my commitment to change my behavior. I am not saying this is an easy process, but it is worth it.

I personally don't call people racist. Instead, I focus on their racist behaviors and attitudes that perpetuate the racist status quo. This is a practical strategy that I find more productive in my work. I believe we all learned and act out of racist stereotypes and prejudice. Our actions maintain racist institutions that advantage whites at the devastating expense of the human rights and humanity of people of color and people who identify as multiracial or biracial.

I want every white person to step up and actively work for racial justice. In my experience, however, if I call white people racist, they immediately become defensive and shut down, and I lose the opportunity to support their further understanding and growth. Additionally, I lose them as potential colleagues and white allies in this work. Therefore, I make a tactical choice to change my approach from calling them racist to focusing on how to help them change the racist attitudes and beliefs that are fueling their racist behaviors. From this stance, most white people eventually feel hope that they can heal from the ravages of their racist socialization to be a useful change agent in the world.

Recently, I have heard many stories from whites about family gatherings where their white family members made blatant racist statements, such as "All Lives Matter!" Or derogatory statements related to people of color and welfare or Affirmative Action. Most of the white people reported feeling stuck and frozen, afraid to engage for fear of escalating the racist dynamics. In addition to the tools and approaches I discussed in Chapter 7, I might respond in these moments by asking a few questions, such as, "I'm trying to remember the first time I heard that statement. Do you remember? I wonder who benefitted from our believing that? Or how we benefit from holding on to that belief today?"

If they seem open to the conversation, I might continue, "Today, I recognize that statement is one of the many racialized messages I was taught that don't serve me any longer. It took a while, but every time I met and got to know another person of color, I had more evidence and life experience to refute the racist stereotypes I bought into. And in those times I still fall back into thinking those statements might be true, I remind myself of other examples and memories that contradict these false generalizations in order to interrupt my racist thoughts. I'm usually able to shift my thinking, which is so ingrained from my life history, to focus more accurately on my truth today. I'm glad to share more about this now or sometime later, if you want." Not every white relative will be open to this conversation, but I believe many will want to talk more, if not in the moment, then over time.

I don't remember doing anything racist these last couple of weeks, but I don't doubt that I will at some point in the near future. It is my daily responsibility to stay awake so I will recognize and interrupt the pervasive racist beliefs around me and inside of me. Instead of worrying so much about being called a racist, I can invest my time, energy, and attention on creating more racially just environments and use my white privilege to intervene to shift racist comments and dynamics in the moment. I can partner with people of color and other white people to address institutional

KATHY OBEAR / 141

racism as we analyze policies, programs, and services with a race lens to identify ways these current practices, possibly unintentionally, still privilege whites and disadvantage people of color through creating unnecessary, inequitable barriers and obstacles to success.

The next time I do something racist, I hope I will trust the process and be present enough to show up in humility as I stay in dialogue with others and with myself. This is a life-long journey to unlearn all the pervasive racist messages I was taught and shift all the lies I learned that whites were smarter and more competent and that white culture is the right and only way to operate within organizations and society.

I believe it is imperative that all white change agents fully embrace their critical role and responsibility to co-create truly inclusive, racially just environments in our organizations and in society. We must continually deepen our own self-work to recognize and release all the racist messages and beliefs we have internalized and that, possibly unconsciously, continue to fuel our actions and perpetuate racism in our daily activities.

We can't do this alone.

I hope you create and nurture a community of white allies to support you and hold you accountable to act on your commitment to create racial justice. My hope is that some of the stories, reflections, and tools in this book will inspire and motivate you to intentionally, consistently, and authentically address issues of race and racism and create liberation in everything you do. I believe that together we can build on the centuries of change and liberation we inherited and leave our legacy as we work towards true justice for all.

I need each and every one of you in this work.

Please do not turn away from this calling just because it's hard or you are afraid. As John F. Kennedy said, "To whom much is given, much is required." We all continue to receive so much unearned white privilege, and I believe it is our moral and ethical responsibility to constantly use these advantages to dismantle racism and racist dynamics wherever we encounter them. In those moments when you are standing at the crossroads between fear and transformation, I hope you always choose courage, take the risk to speak up, and live into your values and vision of a better world.

There may be consequences for living in integrity. It may mean we experience significant backlash from family, colleagues, and supervisors. But as the phenomenal Lin Manuel Miranda said as he portrayed Alexander Hamilton on Broadway, "I'd rather be divisive than indecisive."

Given all the white privilege I receive, whatever problems or challenges I experience when I speak up pale in comparison to what people of color experience every day. And the benefits far outweigh any costs. I get to wake up, look in the mirror, and know that I am doing my part to create greater racial justice and liberation.

"What counts in life is not the mere fact that we have lived. It is what difference we have made to the lives of others that will determine the significance of the life we lead."
- Nelson Mandela

I have a long way to go. But it helps me keep going when I remember how many white people have come before as well as how many are on this road to recovery today. Together, we can reclaim our humanity and live side by side in coalition and in community with people of color as we partner to dismantle racism and white supremacy in every aspect of our lives. I pray you stay on this journey for your own sake and for all of our lives. I hope you choose to live a life of significance and leave a legacy of racial justice for generations to come.

FURTHER READING

Adams, M., & Bell, L. A., (2016). *Teaching for diversity and social justice (3rd ed.)*. New York: Routledge.

Bell, L. A., Funk, M. S., Joshi, K. Y., & Valdivia, M. (2016). Racism and white privilege. In M. Adams, L. A. Bell (Eds.), *Teaching for diversity and social justice (3rd ed.; pp. 133-181)*. New York: Routledge.

Cullen, M. J. (2008). *35 Dumb Things Well-Intended People Say: Surprising Things We Say That Widen the Diversity*. NY: Morgan James.

DiAngelo, R. (2011) White fragility, *International Journal of Critical Pedagogy*, Vol 3 (3), 54-70.

Gant, J. L. (2013). *An educator from Telogia*. Self-published.

Goodman, D. J. (2011). *Promoting diversity and social justice: Educating people from privileged groups. (2nd ed.)*. New York: Routledge.

Harper, S. R. (2011). Strategy and intentionality in practice. In J. H. Schuh, S. R. Jones, & S. R. Harper (Eds.), *Student services: A handbook for the profession* (5th ed.; pp. 287–302). San Francisco: Jossey-Bass.

Irving, D. (2014). *Waking Up White: and Finding Myself in the Story of Race*. Cambridge, MA: Elephant Room Press.

Jackson, B. W. (2005). The theory and practice of multicultural organization development in education. In M. L. Ouellett (Ed.), *Teaching inclusively: Resources for course, department and institutional change in higher education* (pp. 3-20). Stillwater, OK: New Forums Press.

Jackson, B. W. (2006). Theory and practice of multicultural organization development. In Jones, B. & Brazzel, M. (Eds.), *The NTL Handbook of Organization Development and Change* (pps. 139-154). Arlington, VA: NTL Institute.

Jackson, B. W. & Hardiman, R. (1994). Multicultural organization development. In E. Y. Cross, J. H. Katz, F. A. Miller, & E. W. Seashore (Eds.), *The promise of diversity: Over 40 voices discuss strategies for eliminating discrimination in organizations* (pp. 231-239). Arlington, VA: NTL Institute.

Jackson, B. W. and Holvino, E. V. (1988, Fall), Developing multicultural organizations, *Journal of Religion and Applied Behavioral Science* (Association for Creative Change), 14-19.

Johnson, A. G. (2001). *Privilege, Power, and Difference*, Mayfield Publishing.

Kendall, F. (2006). *Understanding White Privilege*, Routledge.

Kivel, P. (2002). *Uprooting Racism: How White People Can Work for Racial Justice*, New Society Publishers.

Marchesani, L. S. and Jackson, B. W. (2005), Transforming higher education institutions using Multicultural Organizational Development: A case study at a large northeastern university. In M. L. Ouellett (Ed.), *Teaching inclusively: Resources for course, department and institutional change in higher education*, 241-257. Stillwater, OK: New Forums Press.

Obear, K. H. (2013). Navigating triggering events: Critical competencies for social justice educators. In L. M. Landreman (Ed.), *The Art of Effective Facilitation: Reflections from Social Justice Educators,* 151-172. Stylus.

Obear, K. H. (2013). *Turn the tide: Rise above toxic, difficult situations in the workplace.* Difference Press.

Obear, K. H. & Kerr, S. (2015). Creating inclusive organizations: One student affairs division's efforts to create sustainable, systemic change. In S. K. Watt (ed.), *Designing Transformative Multicultural Initiatives,* 136-152. Stylus.

Okun, T. (2001). *Dismantling Racism: A Workbook for Social Change Groups.* ChangeWork. http://www.dismantlingracism.org/uploads/4/3/5/7/43579015/whitesupcul13.pdf

Pope, R. L., Reynolds, A. L., and Mueller, J. A. (2004). *Multicultural Competence in Student Affairs.* Jossey-Bass.

Professional Competency Areas for Student Affairs Practitioners, a Joint Publication, ACPA and NASPA, 2010.

Riley, B. E. & Frost, D. D. (2009). *Are you ready for outrageous success?* Lulu.com.

Rothenberg, P. S. (2015). *White privilege: Essential readings on the other side of racism.* New York: Worth Publishing.

Smith, C. *The cost of privilege: Taking on the system of white supremacy and racism.* Fayetteville, NC: Camino Press.

Sue, D. W. (2010). *Microaggressions in everyday life.* Hoboken, NJ: John Wiley & Sons.

Sue, D. W. & Torino, G. C. (2005). "Racial-cultural competence: Awareness, knowledge and skills." In Carter, R. (Ed.), *Handbook of racial-cultural psychology and counseling: Training and practice*, 3-18. Hoboken, NJ: Wiley.

Tatum, B. (1997). *Why Are All the Black Kids Sitting Together in the Cafeteria.* NY: Basic Books.

Tochluk, S. (2010). *Witnessing Whiteness: The Need to Talk About Race and How to Do It* (2nd Ed.). Lanham, MD: Rowman & Littlefield Education.

Washington, J. E. (2012). "Social Justice Education In Higher Education: A Conversation With Rev. Dr. Jamie Washington," Journal of Critical Thought and Praxis: Vol. 1: Issue 1, Article 4.

Wise, Tim (2005). *White Like Me.* Brooklyn, NY: Soft Skull.

ACKNOWLEDGEMENTS

I would not be who I am today without the love, support, and nudges from so many hundreds of people over the years. I would not and could not have written this book but for all the mentors, coaches, and role models who so generously and persistently stayed with me and spurred me on my journey.

For all those who have come before, on whose shoulders I stand: I will never be able to express how profoundly you have changed my life as a white person and those of tens of millions of others. Your sacrifice, courage, and revolutionary spirit ~ your leadership and your partnering with people of color to transform racism and white supremacy have gotten us to this moment. And it is our time to do our part to continue to disrupt and dismantle the oppressive status quo as we create liberation and racial justice for all. And then the next generations will rise and do their part.

I used to believe that we would eradicate racism in my lifetime. And that may still be true, though the recent election gives me grave pause. I choose to believe that we are experiencing the last gasp of those who choose fear, hatred and bigotry as they resist the inevitable reality of our insurmountable tidal wave of light workers, healers, and change agents who will not be moved.

To all my mentors and colleagues in Elsie Y. Cross Associates whom I had the deep honor to learn and work with: I am so profoundly grateful for your love and support and for holding me to a higher standard than I imagined I could reach. All that I learned with you, I carry forward in all my work and my life. I am different today because of you: Elsie Y. Cross, Delyte Frost, Barbara Riley, Shirley Fletcher, Patti Wilson, Toni Dunton, Curt Waller, Jack Gant, Bo Razak, and so many others, thank you.

To Bailey Jackson and Rita Hardiman, thank you for helping me learn how to create systemic institutional change, to move beyond the individual level to mobilize and empower people to create inclusive organizations.

For the other Founding Faculty of the Social Justice Institute (SJTI), Jamie Washington, Vernon Wall and Maura Cullen: I am so deeply grateful for our vision and our collective work to manifest SJTI. And to Becky Martinez for your commitment and leadership to move us into the Next Generation! So much of what I wrote about in this book I learned co-facilitating SJTI. I am deeply grateful for the insights and inspiration I was gifted from the participants in the white caucuses. I have learned and changed so much from the white interns who nudged and supported me as I grew more into myself. And I am so grateful for all the people of color and people who identify as biracial and multiracial who have attended SJTI. I am different today because of you and your courage, your wisdom, your truth.

To my twin puppy, the Rev. Dr. Jamie Washington, I love you soul to soul! I am so grateful for how you persistently, fiercely, and lovingly tell me the truth, hold me accountable, believe I can do better, and walk with me on this journey for all these decades. I am more of me because of you.

To Angela Lauria, Cynthia Kane, and the incredible folks at The Difference Press: I am so deeply grateful for your encouragement to write this book. It was your idea, and I thank you for your vision and seeing what I could not yet envision. Your loving, insightful feedback and coaching helped me birth this book, thank you.

To my love, my beloved, Paulette Dalpes. Thank you for partnering with me on this journey to dismantle white supremacy and racism. Your deep love, support, encouragement, and role modeling fill me up and motivate me to live my calling. I don't know if I would be on this path without you in my life.

And to all those who are rising up now, thank you for teaching me how to organize, protest, and refuse to be complacent and complicit. I honor you and thank you for continuing to energize us all as we do our part to manifest racial justice in ourselves, our organizations, our communities, our world. Together, we rise!

ABOUT THE AUTHOR

Kathy Obear, Ed. D., grew up in mostly all white neighborhoods and schools without realizing how much she absorbed the racist messages of that time. For the first 40 years of her life she believed she was doing her part to create a better world. And then everything changed when she was given very clear feedback that started her on the journey to realize how often she reacted out of the racist attitudes and biases she still held onto.

Kathy has been speaking and training about racism and creating inclusive organizations for over 30 years. As a trainer, consultant, speaker, and coach, she has supported and challenged individuals to lead from where they are and dismantle racist dynamics and practices in themselves and in their organizations.

As Co-Founder and Faculty of the Social Justice Training Institute (SJTI), she continues to develop and inspire the next generations of change agents to speak their truth to power and stand up with courage to create the world they envision. As she facilitates white caucuses at SJTI and in other organizations, she creates the space for whites to heal from the racist and white supremacist messages they were taught and develop the tools to effectively partner with people of color and other whites to create racial justice.

If you are interested in accelerating your capacity to create transformative change in the world, contact her at www.drkathyobear.com/contact.

Kathy lives with her wife of over 30 years and the two amazing kitty muses who helped her complete this book!

Website: www.drkathyobear.com
Email: Kathy@drkathyobear.com
Facebook: https://www.facebook.com/kathy.obear

THANK YOU

Thank you for reading my book! I hope you found a sense of connection and community as well as inspiration to continue on your journey to create racial justice.

To show my appreciation, I want to give you access to two resources: my recent self-assessment, *Suggested Competencies for White Change Agents* and the *Guide to Leading Your Own Book Club*. I hope these tools support your continued development and commitment to create meaningful, sustainable change and greater racial justice in the world. Please visit www.drkathyobear.com/racebook to access these resources.

For information about **working with me to accelerate your capacity to create transformational change in the world,** please visit my website, www.drkathyobear.com or **contact me** directly www.drkathyobear.com/contact.

To schedule a **free 30-minute Strategy Session** to explore the possibility of our working together, use this link www.drkathyobear.com/complimentary-session.

"In two years we've created over 250 bestselling books in a row, 90% from first-time authors." We do this by selecting the highest quality and highest potential applicants for our future programs.

Our program doesn't just teach you how to write a book—our team of coaches, developmental editors, copy editors, art directors, and marketing experts incubate you from book idea to published bestseller, ensuring that the book you create can actually make a difference in the world. Then we give you the training you need to use your book to make the difference you want to make in the world, or to create a business out of serving your readers. If you have life-or world-changing ideas or services, a servant's heart, and the willingness to do what it REALLY takes to make a difference in the world with your book, go to http://theauthorincubator.com/apply/ to complete an application for the program today.

Help! My Kid Wants to Become a Youtuber

by Michael Buckley and Jess Malhotra

...But I'm Not Racist!: Tools for Well-Meaning Whites

by Kathy Obear

Pride: You Can't Heal If You're Hiding from Yourself

by Ron Holt

The Face of the Business: Develop Your Signature Style, Step Out from Behind the Curtain and Catapult Your Business on Video

by Rachel Nachmias

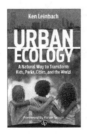

Urban Ecology: A Natural Way to Transform Kids, Parks, Cities, and the World

by Ken Leinbach

Why Can't I Drink Like Everyone Else?: A Step-By-Step Guide to Understanding Why You Drink and Knowing How to Take a Break

by Rachel Hart

Finding Time to Lead: Seven Practices to Unleash Outrageous Potential

by Leslie Peters

Standing Up: From Renegade Professor to Middle-Aged Comic

by Ada Cheng

Flex Mom: The Secrets of Happy Stay-At-Home Moms

by Sara Blanchard

Your First CFO: The Accounting Cure for Small Business Owners

by Pam Prior

Just Tell Me What I Want: How to Find Your Purpose When You Have No Idea What It Is

by Sara Kravitz

From Sidelines to Start Lines: The Frustrated Runner's Guide to Lacing Up for a Lifetime

by Sarah Richardson

Everyday Medium: 7 Steps to Discover, Develop and Direct Your Sixth Sense

by Marsha Farias

Think Again!: Clearing Away the Brain Fog of Menopause

by Jeanne Andrus

Relationship Detox: 7 Steps to Prepare for Your Ideal Relationship

by Jodi Schuelke

Unclutter Your Spirit: How Your Stuff is a Treasure Map to Your Inner Wisdom

by Sue Rasmussed